Fools, Bells, and the Habit of Eating
Three Satires

Zakes Mda

WITS UNIVERSITY PRESS

Witwatersrand University Press
1 Jan Smuts Avenue
Johannesburg
2001
South Africa

ISBN 978 1 8681 4377 1

© Zakes Mda
© Introduction: Rob Amato

All rights reserved. No part of this publication may be reproduced, stored
in a retrieval system, or transmitted in any form or by any means, electronic,
mechanical, photocopying, recording or otherwise, without the prior
permission of the copyright owners.

First published 2002
Second printing 2004
Third printing 2016

Applications to perform these works in public should be directed to:
DALRO
P.O. Box 9292
Johannesburg
2000
South Africa

Cover photograph: Jean van Lingen, Amsterdam

Cover Design and Typesetting by Crazy Cat Designs,
Johannesburg, South Africa
Printed and bound by ABC Press, Cape Town

Contents

Zakes Mda

Introduction

Rob Amato

Mdada *(n), also* **Mdada-ism:** elusive black theatrical satire in the old and new Southern Africa.

Zakes Mda has a fiercely independent critical mind, always shifting its perspectives, always ready for a more-than-real theatricality. His best playwriting is unavoidably provocative, and often works through forcing an improbable set of assumptions upon the audience — strangeness is his friend. One is only some of the time quite sure what is being satirised. Opposing but valid interpretations come easily off his pages to actors and directors, who can often play something two or three ways. Mda's theatricality is both African and modern, it often invites the adjective 'surreal' but that word does not easily match the usually perfectly logical argument of the pieces. The plays often turn on a sadness or grotesquerie, some painful and ironic turn of history that has been, is, or will become important, perhaps ten years ahead of the time it is written about. The work has often been prophetic.

Earlier Plays

In the 1970s Mda offered three very disparate plays presented at the People's Space and Market Theatres. The dates are important — each play comes in a different political atmosphere. *Dark Voices Ring* (1976, the time of the Soweto student uprising) was a clarion call for revolution presented by a fiery young warrior and his deeply angry mother. They prepare themselves for the coming liberation war with song and the oratory of the oppressed, while his incapacitated father watches in silence, smiling only at the end of the play when the youth departs for the north to change the world. Little irony here, but hypnotic portraits. Archetypes: the liberation warrior, played at the People's Space by Fitzroy Ncgukana, and his agonised, powerful, harsh-voiced mother, played by Nomhle Nkonyeni, South Africa's dark powerhouse tragic actress.

We Shall Sing for the Fatherland (1976/7 when everyone else was doing revolutionary as opposed to protest theatre) was, as it were, written in the opposite direction, that of the mocking disbeliever in revolutions in the real world. Created from a perspective different from that chosen by many black South African writers of the time (Mda has always appreciated that black regimes can be as rotten as white) it presents two maimed ex-soldiers, now park-dwelling bums, who are patronised and abandoned by the callous generals, business people and politicians of a 'successful' liberation movement in an un-named country. The veterans are both comic and tragic. Naive spokespeople for those who think that just rewards come to those who sacrifice life and limb for them, they are also battered examples of an opposing reality. In the real South Africa, after the 1994 democratic elections, many Umkhonto we Sizwe (Spear of the Nation) soldiers were taken into the new integrated South African defence force but almost as many (the rougher soldiers who drink and are undisciplined) became real-life embodiments of Mda's ragged African veterans, abandoned in parks. In Zimbabwe (South Africa's troubled northern neighbour) some of the same archetypical war veterans now kill life-long workers on white Zimbabwean farms, accusing them of selling out or of voting for the moderate Movement for Democratic Change.

The Hill, mounted in 1977/8, when black piety and martyrdom were becoming set patterns in theatre, was Mda's mordant portrait of Maseru, the capital of Lesotho, as a refuge for randy South African white men, a place of porn movies, whores and poverty, of nearly glitzy hotels and local black women dealing very effectively (if sadly) with being 'left behind' by migrant male mineworkers. Lesotho, an independent Kingdom, has always served as a pool of labour for South Africa, which entirely surrounds it.

The play's title refers to the wild hill in Maseru above the recruiting offices of the South African gold mines. There, in proximity to the local Hilton Hotel, men in traditional blankets wait to be swooped up into the money-promising exploitation of the city of gold. A young dreamer who carries a disconnected steering wheel thinks he will end up with a car full of girls in swaggering Johannesburg. A sweet old veteran of the mines tries futilely to disabuse him. They are joined by a huge, vibrant returning miner (Joko Scott was rampant in the part) who has nothing on but a shirt and underpants and no possessions other than a great empty suitcase, or trunk, which he wields to defend himself. He has been stripped of everything he gained at the mines by the high-heeled whores of Maseru, who follow him onto the stage and proceed to take over the play with their songs, sentimentality and general mayhem.

The play is intensely bittersweet. Mda's affection and pitying scorn alternate powerfully. It has a strange opening image, not picked up again but haunting the play and setting a surreal tone. The piece begins with a nun praying her *mea culpa* in a shadowy, otherworldly cemetery. The (open-ended) frame of the play is thus pious while its body indulges rampant energy and egotism that echoes Ben Jonson. As we produced it for the People's Space *The Hill* was a highly coloured music-filled ironic romp, lit in the garish colours of a fantasy-cum-nightmare. The whores sang sweet Beatles songs between terrorising the men. The piece played a half-hour longer at Roma University, near Maseru, than it did at the People's Space, because the local audience rocked about so long and so loudly at so many lines that the actors could only stand there, waiting. The awful comic truthfulness of the play's lampoonings of Maseru and its ubiquitous whores combined uproariously with the strange effect of its being performed not by Sothos but by a bunch of Xhosas from the Cape. The freshness to the all-black Lesotho audience of the form of satirical musical comedy combined with the intensely recognisable action and created what I describe as Mdada theatre. Truthful exaggeration is a phrase that comes to mind. I can vouch for the truthfulness of the play's characterisation of the whores. One bright morning coming down in the lift in the Holiday Inn I became aware that the woman on my left was projecting silent fury at the safari-suited, navel-showing white farmer on my right, whose emotions were less clear but just as intense. The lift door opened and they went out into the car park dotted with bushes and trees. She whistled once and in a moment the farmer was surrounded by women of undoubted strength who wielded their high stiletto heels. He emptied his wallet, leaped into his Merc and roared off back into the Orange Free State (the South African Province adjacent to Lesotho).

That night, setting up the show at Roma's hall, I came out to fetch some stage lights from my car. It was occupied by four women who made me several offers in remarkably imperious tones. They refused to emerge — I had to leave them in the car. I don't know if they saw the show. My car was still there when the onstage reproduction of those women was over.

Dankie Auntie emerges from the late 1980s, a period in which detention and torture had become endemic under the states of emergency declared by the PW Botha government. Again there is a strong and passionate element of dream. The setting is Hazel, a Karoo town through which the outside world passes only in the form of trains filled with foreign tourists, local soldiers or migrant workers. The heroine is Pearly Heavens, a girl of about nine, who is being interrogated by a sadistic security man (done on stage only by voice and once by shadow) who whips her buttocks (offstage) and tries to extract information useful to the apartheid state from her hopscotch games and fairy stories. Pearly's spirit is seemingly indomitable and she is saved — until the last moments of the play — by her flashback memories of her fellow children, Grand Ou Dame, a fairy-story-witch-cum-spirit-of-Mother-Africa, and Papa Oupa, a ragged songman of ambiguous virtue. Passing trains are a source of coal and food from the hampers of travellers, but the state's bullyboys whip the children away from the line. Pearly dreams of an apple being thrown to her, an apple that contains a diamond.

The story the children get from GOD (the Grand Ou Dame) is that of the King's Flies. The King lives in an exclusive suburb where he has a nice palace and happy courtiers. In the ghetto he has a piggery and fowl run. The flies from these land on the eyes of the children and there is sickness in the land. When the subjects complain the King demands proof that the flies are from his pigs and fowls.

'Catch me just one fly' he said 'that has blue blood. Then only then will I agree they are the King's flies.'

This story haunts the children. They are invited to supply the end. One child thinks that everyone died, but our Pearly, the child-revolutionary, has it that the people got the King and all the courtiers drunk, and then killed all the pigs and chickens and no-one died in the land. The children mock her for this and for her dream of being thrown a diamond in an apple. The Blue Train (the luxury train of South Africa) passes and passengers throw out bits of food. The children cry 'Dankie Auntie!' but we shift back to the interrogation by the torturer who swears he loves Pearly even as he moves to give her electric shocks. In her delirium the children reappear, asking Pearly what the subjects of the King will eat when she has killed all the King's birds and beasts?

Pearly replies:

I could say
Let them eat ice cream
Let them eat candy
But listen, it is true,
From their sweat
Came the King's birds and beasts
And the King's cabbages
From their sweat
Their own will come.

Here Mdada is decidedly Brechtian.

One of the trains which passes is filled with black soldiers who throw cans of beer used as missiles, and the children have to understand that people who look like them are acting like their enemies. But the climactic scene has yet another train from which are thrown objects the children gather, which turn out to be hand grenades. Pearly is still in her cell, and she returns to childishness when the security man calls her her own jailer because of the revolutionary meanings of her dreams. She cries. 'I want my doll back! I want my doll back!'. End of play.

This painful work, that uses children's honesty and imagination but works out Mda's late-eighties fury, is, I think, informed by his experiences in Nicaragua and elsewhere, which were reflected in other plays not traced here. This was Mda's most anti-capitalist period (to date).

Plays after 2 February 1990,
(the date on which the ANC was unbanned)

The Mother of All Eating (1992) is a one-hander. The play has, as its unnamed protagonist, the Man, a Lesotho official who has 'eaten' (his sardonic word for living high on corruption) incessantly in the years preceding the time of the play. What we watch is (almost) one long, blackly humorous but unself-consciously unctuous justification of selfish roguery.

The Man has a remarkable way of summarising the strangely inverted world of aid and foreign investment and prides himself on his ability to escape punishment for taking bribes. He always escapes because everyone else is in on the scene, except his friend Joe, whom he also plays, despisingly, contemptuously, as the honest fool of the play. For everyone else who is threatened with exposure for corruption the one sure escape is to quieten one's threatener with a bribe. But our Man gets his dreadful come-uppance in the play and he has to become human before we leave him, covered in real grief and terror — grief at his pregnant wife's fate in an accident on the very road he has been fraudulently surfacing, papering over, as it were, and terror at his own impending destruction.

This play follows a pattern in Mda's work in that the scheming, living and dreaming impulses of the main character give it its drive. But this Man is immoral, a defender of a thoroughly utilitarian pragmatism, not an innocent. His dreams are there, but for the first time in Mda they are those of an indecent sensibility.

This is a grinding satire on materialism and 'realism' of the cynical kind — 'get-real-ism', if you will. But it ends more 'justly' than the others. We are sledgehammered by all the arguments about the inevitability of corruption until we watch the Man's near-tragic disintegration and despair. In this way *The Mother of All Eating* recalls Marlowe's *Dr Faustus*. We come near to wishing the Man success because we are taken up by his vigour, his intellectual agility, and his selfish nonsense.

Next came *You Fool, How Can the Sky Fall?* 1995, an unbridled study in grotesquerie. On stage in a surreal prison kept by some monstrous force that fingers them to drag themselves out for torture every now and then is a complete Cabinet, a President and his ministers.

Mda believes that government by those who have made a successful revolution is almost inevitably, in the first decade or two, hi-jacked by the smart operators, who ensure that they, and not the people, and especially not the women, are the beneficiaries.

This theme is present in virtually all his work. Mda is interested in many of the ideas of Steve Biko, the martyred Black Consciousness leader who wrote what he liked and stressed self-reliance above all things. Along with Mda's theatrical questioning of post-revolutionary governments and grotesque/heroic individual political types (which is his own, not Biko's, territory) goes a Biko-like demand, made also by Mda the man himself in interviews, that people should not expect governments to feed and support them.

But one should not stress the mundane analytical and abstracted language of interview politics in talking of Mdadaism. Nor is it simply right to talk of it as surrealism, though it has many of its traits. Mda works theatre in a way that reflects the usually invisible or inarticulated obscurities of the black southern African sensibility. His plays may be informed by European surrealist techniques and styles (like Dadaism) but they are minute-to-minute African, in fusions which are accessible to modern blacks. There is a deep logic, and I suspect there is nary a moment of his plays in performance which causes a black or white South African audience to reject their conventions or fail to follow or at least accept their often dream-based logic. Mdadaism is South Africa dreaming, a force which invades and reveals South African reality.

Neil Sonnekus, a writer who did a playwright's workshop with Mda, has remarked that talk of surrealism irritated the man. Sonnekus remembers him arguing 'quiveringly' that for Africans dream and reality were two parts of reality. One habitually regarded one's dreams as serious evidence of the nature of one's being, and one's fate. The nightmare of *You Fool, How can the Sky Fall?* is based on gross exaggeration of a real set of possibilities.

> AGRICULTURE [*after the woman Minister of Health has dragged herself off at the silent summons of the un-named offstage torturer who throws open a clanking door and rattles chains and keys periodically through the play, for another victim from the Cabinet to go off to be tortured.*]: Anyway, that's going to teach her a thing or two. She'll know that being a minister is not all fun and games. I bet when she comes back she'll know how to eat humble pie ...
> PRESIDENT: The disadvantages of having her here are far outweighed by the benefits we'll reap from her presence.
> AGRICULTURE: They are slow in coming, these benefits, Wise One. The Daughters of the Revolution continue to be a nuisance.
> CULTURE: So that is why she was made a minister, to control the Daughters of the Revolution?
> PRESIDENT: We made her a minister as an indication that we are an enlightened government. The fact that that would silence the Daughters of the Revolution by showing them we had a woman in the Cabinet was supposed only to be the icing on our cake. A by-product of our enlightenment.
> JUSTICE: Our plan didn't work then. The Daughters of the Revolution are still at it. She should have reverted to her womanly role after the revolution.
> PRESIDENT: They are at it again?

AGRICULTURE: Demonstrating and polluting this whole city with the stench of filthy ideas.

JUSTICE: Like the stench of the buckets of faeces in this cell.

AGRICULTURE: At least we live with it here, and we are so used to it that if it were not here we would all get sick ...

JUSTICE: We should have been ruthless right from the beginning. Justice can only be served through ruthlessness. We inherited this revolution from those who did the actual fighting. We now own it. They refuse to accept that at their peril.

AGRICULTURE [*laughing*]: They have now taken to marching naked at the Market Square ...

This (in addition to its mordant satire) is another example of Mda (or Mdada) in symbolic prophecy mode. In 2001 many large South African black women, protesting at the (horribly retrospective) state destruction of their squatter shelters during the Bredell land occupations, did indeed sing their protest songs in the nude. In the world of the play this rebellious nudity makes men flee because it can render them blind. In the world of present day South Africa it made very surreal cover photos for *The Sowetan*, a Johannesburg newspaper with a largely black readership.

I suspect that Mda is a satirical, 'magical realist', post-modernist, post-structuralist, post-deconstructionist version of Credo Mutwa, the literary *sangoma* (diviner) who, with Blake-like assurance, invents cosmologies and mythologies for his own purposes, implying them to be old and African. Who knows what in this play comes from where? Clearly most of it comes from the fairly commonplace satirical idea of the modern African Cabinet seen as a collection of self-serving, morally bankrupt rhetoric-mongers who do nothing but vie for power, cover their backs, and lust. But there are mysterious *pitiki* dances, which the Cabinet believes will unseat them. Unseat them from what? They talk as if they are still in power, but we watch them confined to a filthy prison. Only at the last moment do we get an explanation of this, cleverly and (almost) convincingly based on the concretisation of presidential psychosis.

How may this brilliantly horrible comedy work on stage? First, my armchair would-be director's reading and then some reviews of its production in 1995 at Johannesburg's Windybrow Theatre.

You Fool demands a Fellini of a director because the actors must convey outrageously extreme Bosch-like types in various stages of terror, delusion and grandiloquent lunacy. The play must hurtle along.

And the style must stink of decayed old Europe and corrupt new Africa, from the 'old master' tableau at the beginning through the Latinate language ('defecate', 'fornicate', never a swear-word in an atmosphere where flies, cockroaches and black widow spiders provide the imagery) to a hypnotic use of dance that has a St Vitus quality. There are, in the presidential rituals, echoes of the medieval King's Chamber — the public Royal Undressing and Morning Rising. People drag *themselves* offstage screaming and protesting. There is much direct lambasting of the philistinism of the typical modern African government with its badly disguised contempt for things cultural. (This is spiced by the Minister of Culture complaining at having to deal with country dancers when he'd prefer to get comebacks from bridge construction projects. He is also a bad and mercenary poet who tries, unsuccessfully in spite of his position, to have his poetry prescribed at schools.)

There are one or two possibly serious (by which I mean, I suppose, earnest) passages in the play: first a hymn to the eternity of great poetry, then the shrapnel-scarred Daughters of the Revolution demanding memory and restitution. But we return swiftly to grotesquerie. The Minister of Justice is, as in Orwell, the murderous enemy of youth, of dance, and of love. The Young Man, who never sleeps because of what he has seen and because he fears he will wake up blind, is also the unpaid painter of innumerable official portraits of the smiling Cabinet. The female Minister of Health admires the practices of black widow spiders and cheerfully anticipates the coming of the disposable male. The smiling President, who has decreed benevolence while hanging opponents, is terrified by a beauty contest (whose terror lies partly in that it has *already happened!)* won by an old, old woman who carries her shrapnel scars with pride.

The humour runs from the literary/analytic:

> PRESIDENT: They want our heads on a platter.
> YOUNG MAN: They have tried to eat symbols but they still remain hungry.
> To the throwaway turnaround:
> CULTURE: Who's going to do it [*give the President a doctorate*]? The Honourable the Minister of Education is not here.
> HEALTH: You can do it. Your ministry is closest to his.
> JUSTICE [*who hates* CULTURE *with a fierce, contemptuous jealousy*]: You can't give such great responsibility to him.
> CULTURE: And why not?
> YOUNG MAN: Yes, why not?
> JUSTICE: Okay. Just do it then.

There is talk, whose tone is inscrutable, about the 'theatre of rebirth' which may be earnestly or satirically connected to the 'African Renaissance'.

It is commonly held that no-one knows or can determine Shakespeare's politics or religion, not even at specific stages of his writing career. It is his characters, not he, who have passions and ideas. So it is, nearly all the time, with Mda as playwright. He is at his best when he unsettles the world, not when he argues a case. Mdada is not easily placed. In *You Fool, How Can the Sky Fall?* the playwright Mda deals explicitly, if ambiguously, with the idea that all truth, especially passionate truth, is ephemeral, 'the truth of the day'. This relativist position is characteristic of our sophisticated times, but it doesn't, in Mdada, remove obligations. Peter Se-Puma, director of the 1995 production, connects the play's point about changing truths to our own responsibilites, which are not stressed by European surrealists. Mdada, unlike Dada, is not embarassed by didacticism. Se-Puma says: 'The truths of today that we die for may tomorrow be lies, and we would have only ourselves to blame.'[1]

---

[1] *City Press*, 5 February 1995.

There are several dry truths, mouthed by characters, which may be eternal:

> YOUNG MAN: When the ruling classes disagree they don't kill one another, they joke about their disagreements at cocktail parties, while we murder each other about those very disagreements.

One of the play's nastier ideas is that there are people, emotional ghouls, who use make-up to pretend they have scars and lacerations. Make-up on stage and make-up in the story become one, both are self-pitying, self-indulging disguises, phony wounds for phony martyrdom. This play is one whose real virtues and vices will emerge only in very gifted performance and direction. This is not to say that the armchair director, the reader of the text, hasn't got plenty to think about and respond to, but that's harder than watching a developed 'reading' on stage. The strange question is whether the audience at a strong performance can see behind the reading to the alternative readings. The great refreshment that Zakes Mda gives to South African theatre is precisely in this area. There is always space for the mysterious play-mind, the play's mind, beyond Zakes Mda's mind. This play's mind (an essential part of Mdada) is always ready to be influenced by all the subtle variants, as numerous (and as easily processable by the directorial mind) as pixels in a digital photograph. The process of manipulating the theatrical pixels is analogous to playing with an image in Photoshop. Each unified distortion gives each moment a different meaning controlled by an overall formula. These minuscule elements make the performed play itself, but they arise out of its demands when conceived by the playwright at the desk, its wonderful nonsense, *its* organic, amoral being.

Director Peter Se-Puma is quoted[2] as saying that it took him three readings of the play to realise that it was a refreshingly new type of play for South Africa.

> Some moments appear quite normal, but then the next moment abnormal things occur so the deliberate absurdity makes it easier for audiences to relate to what's in the play in a realistic way.

---

[2] *Ibid*

In an admiring review[3] headlined 'Be back soon. Wait: Godot' Garalt MacLiam saw the work as part satire, part parable, and noted the links to Samuel Beckett and Harold Pinter. He praised the director for picking up on the *logical* nature of what I'm calling Mdada.

> It is to the benefit of the audience that illogical apects of the proceedings are given an acceptable logicality by Peter Se-Puma through the calculated introduction of moments of tension.

I cannot, of course, be sure but I suspect that virtually all the tension and logic that Se Puma elicited from this fertile text was implicit in it. MacLiam gives insight into Shuping Shuping's design:

> *You Fool* was performed with audiences on either side of an ellipse and the result is that none of the play's characters can hide from the penetrating gaze of the collective, or such is the illusion created.

The first production cast a white woman, Theresa Iglich, as the Minister of Health, whom MacLiam describes as 'quite off the wall' and as being 'overtaken by a sexual euphoria which will hold her helpless in its thrall' whenever the unseen Minister of Works is mentioned. It also had the General played by an extremely expressive white actor, Anton Dekker. This must have reverberated in February 1995, when the first South African Cabinet to be mixed in race (and gender) was barely a year old. The contrast must have been palpable between Mandela and the 'bantam president' (Gamakhula Diniso) of the production who, for Macliam, 'struts and bobs as he imposes his will on his colleagues, sometimes subtly, sometimes by overt threat'.

Mfundo Ndebele in the *New Nation*[4] remarked on Diniso's mixture of impish charm and imperiousness. He saw the play as a searing indictment of dictatorship that 'veers between tense and dramatic scenes — where the horrors of arbitrary arrest and torture are powerfully and convincingly evoked — to moments of side-splitting farce.'

The Bells of Amersfoort (2002) is a musical piece which Mda, in a note to the publishers, describes as

---

[3] *The Star*, 13 February 1995.
[4] 17 February 1995.

the most recent of my plays. It tries to rehabilitate the Afrikaner in the imagination of South Africa. An Afrikaner man, who was the oppressor and the torturer in the old South Africa, becomes the key element in the development of the country and in rebuilding it in the new South Africa. When the former 'comrade' decides to take the route of unbridled accumulation of wealth in the so-called black empowerment frenzy, the black woman and the Afrikaner man go to 'heal the land'.

The story in this play is told in the manner of the Xhosa traditional theatre known as Intsomi. Scene 12, especially, uses the Intsomi storytelling devices, with the woman asking grotesque figures questions about her lover, and the figures punctuating their responses with an Intsomi song in the same manner as it would be told by storytellers around the fire in the evening.

The piece uses several Mdadaist methods. It demands three acting areas, called the first, second and third worlds in the stage directions. These are not the expected political or geographic domains that the phrasing suggests. The first world is the room in Amersfoort where Tami Walaza presently lives alone except for visits from Katja, a beautiful Dutch girl who tries to lift her from her exiled depression. Tami is depressed and sinking into alcoholism, but she plays the trombone. She reacts to the bells of the church in Amersfoort as if she were being physically tortured by the sound. From this world she communicates either by telepathy or actual letters with her former lover Luthando Vela who appears in the second world, the South African world she has left behind, which is also the world to which she will return. We are given conflicting signals on the nature of the communication, which sometimes seems telepathic and spiritual and sometimes ordinary and factual.

Here is a significant stage direction: 'The third world is the world she will never reach, the world she observes from her window. She vicariously participates in this world as well, although it unfolds across the street.'

To that world comes a South African dominee who, following the tradition of his church, is studying theology in Holland. He is also making spectacular, theatrical love to Heleen, a black prostitute. They don't draw the curtains. Tami finds solace in watching them and ends up providing the music for their weekly trysts, accompanied by a band of friends.

The main movement of the play is towards an improbable and yet in many ways convincing further liberation of South Africans in Amersfoort and, by implication, back home. Tami comes to realise that the comrade she was going to marry in the old South Africa is now a profoundly corrupt powermonger in the new republic, and moves her attention, if not yet her affections, to the white Afrikaner man who tortured her in the old regime — the dominee who had worked for the old security forces. The tale is made warm and yet not cloying by its sexual frankness, its openness to the magic of song and to Mdadaist theatricality — wire cars and bicycles, a child-like element of play blending with mystic Africanism and modern carnal romance. It will demand a strange mixture of innocence and sophistication in performance and should, as it unfolds, become a rare vehicle for the fusion of Dutch and Xhosa musical and theatrical conventions.

So what is Mdada? I derive it, describe it, from a process I joined more than twenty years ago as the first production director of *Dark Voices Ring* and *The Hill*, and from looking at the other plays introduced here as I would if commissioned to direct them. Mdada is an art that encourages the mind to allow itself licence to many freedoms which are unique to live theatre, and in some of their aspects, to South African theatre.

Why only in the live theatre? Because the theatre (when used by an instinctually theatrical writer like Mda) creates answerability to the moment and its meanings, an answerability that arises out of a chain (which must form a complete circle) of irreplaceable *doers*. When such theatre works, which it seems is rarer and rarer, it reflects:

- The playwright, as servant of the people of the play and yet as arbiter of the society. He has two primary roles — to transmit the human into lines and action for actors, and to create, by selection and the logic of design, the magic box which allows everyone — director, actors, musicians, dancers, audience — to play with the characters and their interactions. He is the storyteller/dream merchant who carries forward the mythical world, so that it passes the present world and implies the future world.

- The director, whose first artistic decisions are casting decisions, whose stylistic decisions are multi-faceted, and who sets up the polarities of analysis which the production will engage. He is catalyst rather than judge, and a good director of Mdadaist theatre will open possible readings rather than restrict them.

- The actors, each of whom is both servant and creator of the character, occupied as a city gets occupied. Sometimes the character behaves as the occupier wants; sometimes it reverts to the city it was before occupation.

- The actors as dancers or musicians. These *form-people* (the dance-person, the trombone-person, the percussion-person, the sung vocal-person, all as opposed to the-word-spoken—naturally-in-a-mimicked-character-person) gain genre-based powers that should often be brought to bear on the analytic excitements of Mdadaist theatre.

And, most important,

- The audience, whose primary function is moment-to-moment *assessment* of the artistry of the play, the characters, the ideas and the arguments. Theatre practitioners, thrashed into the mind-set dictated by bums-on-seats calculations, nearly always believe the primary function of the audience is to be entertained, to have its attention compelled. In Mdadaist theatre entertainment is the essential by-product. The primary invitation is to *assess* as one gets pulled along by actor-embodied comedy and anguish, not by evidence as it might be on the page or in a court of law. And of course the audience in Mdada is as much an actor as the actors.

One Mdadaist rule: The psychic self-reliance of the artist means he cannot be in the swim of things, doing what's been done before. He must walk — or swim — ahead.

Another: Be elusive.

Another: Be unlikely to come quickly to one or even to two or three conclusions. Seek to be a newcomer to your own city, just starting the games that must be played there.

Another: Play.

The Mother
of All Eating

The Mother of All Eating was first performed at the Sechaba Hall, Victoria Hotel, Maseru, Lesotho, on 12 March 1992 with Gonzalez Mosiuoa Scout as The Man.

The play was directed by Zakes Mda

Scene One

Music, guitar and drums. Lights rise. There are two chairs on the stage which is otherwise devoid of sets. Humming outside. A knock. Another knock. THE MAN walks in. He is an executive type in a business suit. He holds a briefcase.

THE MAN: Honey, I am home! Now where is she? Hello! Honey! I am home!

He looks around the room, but 'honey' is nowhere to be seen.

THE MAN: Where can she be? She hasn't even left me a note. [*Laughs.*] A 'dear John' note perhaps. [*Laughs.*] Not on your life. We have a good life together. You know, I have been fortunate in many respects, and I never stop counting my blessings, especially as far as she is concerned.

The phone rings. He lifts the receiver.

THE MAN: Hello! Oh, it's you, Jane. No, she is not here. I thought she was with you, as a matter of fact ... Oh, my God, I wonder where she's gone to, particularly at this time of the night ... Well I have just walked in ... From Johannesburg ... By plane, yes ... Well, the plane was delayed ... A very strange thing happened on the way from Johannesburg. I will tell you all about it this weekend. You are coming to dinner, aren't you? ... How's your man ? ... How many men do you have then ? ... I mean Joe, your husband. You know, Jane, I think Joe has a lot to learn about life ... Yes, I sing about that every day. I will not stop pestering you two about the way you conduct your lives, or misconduct your lives. That's what friends are for, and frankly I am very much concerned. This life is not for playing with. If he wants to mess up his life he must not drag you along with him. You deserve much better. The best things in life, like all the other women of our class ... Jane, I know we have been over that many times before ... But I always hope that one day you will see the light ... Anyway, give me Joe. I want to talk with him ... What? He's not there, and you have no idea where he's gone to? ... So I see, you went to the salon to braid your hair, and when you came back he was not at home ... Well, maybe he's gone down to the pub for a beer ... What do you mean he never drinks during the week? Are you talking of a different Joe from the one I know? My mate for decades, with whom I went to high school and to university? Is this a wishful invention of a new Joe with the virtues of a monk? Even monks have wine cellars ... [*Laughs.*] Well, my wife has disappeared too. I come back from a business trip in Johannesburg and she is not here. [*Laughs.*] Maybe she and Joe eloped, in which case we must also set up house together. Swopping is not a bad idea at all. [*Laughs for a long time.*] ... Of course I am kidding ... Well, Jane, okay man. I will talk with you again tomorrow. I have a lot of paperwork to do before I go to bed. Bye now!

He replaces the receiver, sighs deeply, and smiles to himself.

THE MAN: Jane! My God! What a girl! I really don't know how a fine woman like Jane ends up with a fool like Joe. I mean, Jane ... Well, don't get me wrong. Of course I have lusted after her. Just harmless lust, you understand? I would not have designs on my friend's wife, would I now?

Ha! She says Joe drinks only on weekends. Who does she think she is kidding? Joe drinks like a fish every day — ever since he lost his job. He's been losing one job after another. All because he claims he's principled. That's what happens to people who are principled. They lose their jobs. Joe has a lot to learn about life, I tell you. I am sure right now he's in some shebeen or third rate pub drowning his principled arse in a quart of beer someone else has paid for.

He is getting worried.

THE MAN: My God, it is getting late, and my wife is not home. Where the hell can she be at this hour? And she is not well, you know? She is having a difficult pregnancy. Our first child. After ten years of trying. We are both looking forward to it.

She shouldn't be moving around so late with my baby kicking in her stomach.

He opens the briefcase and examines the papers.

THE MAN: Perhaps I should look at these documents. It is very important that by tomorrow I must be able to present His Excellency the Honourable Minister with all the figures. Of course he won't understand them. He never understands anything. That's why he is a minister and I am his principal secretary. I am supposed to guide him, lead him through the steps. I must be careful though not to lead him completely out of ignorance. Otherwise he'll be too wise, and will demand to read the documents before he signs them. And there is nothing as dangerous as a minister who reads the documents before he signs them. It is for the good of the country that honourable ministers should stay illiterate. Now you see all these documents with all these figures. This is an annexure to an important contract for the construction of a road to the site of our new hydro-electric project. What would happen to our national security if our ministers could read and understand them? Think, my friends! Think! What would happen to our well-being if ministers could read and understand? I leave you with that homework. Right now all I want is to do these figures, to readjust them according to our new agreement with the contractor ... Well, my new agreement, because this is between the contractor and myself. First thing in the morning I must take these documents to His Excellency the Honourable Minister for his signature. Then the deal is clinched between the contractor in Johannesburg and myself. And all this I could have done and completed this afternoon, if the stupid plane had not been delayed.

I could have arrived here at 2 o'clock. It's only an hour from Johannesburg. Indeed the plane did get here at two, but it could not land. There was a hell of a storm, so it could not land. It then had to fly to Bloemfontein, and landed at the airport there. We had to wait for the storm to subside before we could fly back here. The message came that the storm was over, but then the plane had run out of fuel. The pilot was busy trying to negotiate with the airport authorities to fill the plane up with fuel and charge our Great National Airline. But the airport authorities said nothing doing. 'We have given your Great National Airline fuel on credit before, and up to this day we have not been paid. And that was months or even years ago. We shall only give you fuel if you pay cash. No cheque either, but cash.' The pilot, obviously, did not have that kind of cash with him. And in the meantime the passengers were just sitting there, for hours on end, waiting for the problem to be resolved. The day was saved by one of the passengers who happened to have enough cash in his pocket. Well, at last they filled the plane up, and we got to Maseru. That's why I arrived here so late. And here I find my wife has disappeared into thin air.

Come to think of it, this is not the first inconvenience I have suffered with our Great National Airline. On domestic flights I have often arrived late, sometimes eight hours late, at my destination. Once I actually complained after I had missed an important appointment with a contractor I was supposed to meet at a construction site in the mountains. When I came back I complained and was glibly told by a senior official, 'You must be grateful that you arrived at all.'

He puts all the documents in his briefcase and closes it.

THE MAN: Well, I think I must go to my study and work on these documents.

He walks out. Guitar and drum music for about two minutes.

Scene Two

There is a rude knock. THE MAN *comes rushing in.*

THE MAN: Okay! Okay! I am opening. Who can it be who knocks like a policeman?

He opens an imaginary door.

THE MAN: What is it? What do you want from me? ... Now listen, it is late. Can't we talk about this tomorrow? Please ... No, you can't come in now ... Listen, man, I don't have time to discuss this with you. I have a lot of paperwork to do ... Some figures about the new road to the big hydroelectric project ... Of course I know you are the chief engineer in my ministry, but this has nothing to do with you. I am not getting anything out of this. It's a straight and honest deal between the government and the contractor from France. Listen, man, I have many problems now. The paperwork. And it is late at night, and I don't know where my wife is. Can't we discuss this tomorrow? ... What do you mean I am a thief and a crook? ... Listen, you can't come to my house and start hurling insults at me. I tell you I won't stand for it ... You say you want your share, but I tell you I haven't got the money ... The contractor turned against his word after we had given him the contract ... No, no he never deposited the money into my Swiss bank account ... Okay, okay, he deposited a little money. Very little. That's why I was able to give you a coupla thousand. I cannot give you more than that. I have to share with my minister as well, you know ... Listen, don't call me a liar, man. Not in my house ... Shhh, don't shout! Do you want people to hear what we are talking about? Anyway what's the idea of invading me at this time of the night? ... Surely we can talk tomorrow, can't we? Your office is just opposite mine at the ministry. Pop in some time and we can talk in a civilised manner ... No, it is not true that my office is bugged. And my messenger does not spy for ... Well, we'll talk outside then since you are so sure that it is bugged, and walls have ears ... Don't bother me now. Just go in peace and we'll settle everything tomorrow ... What do you mean I haven't heard the last of you? Are you threatening me? Me, your boss, the Principal Secretary of His Majesty's Government? ... Well, just go and sleep and stop being childish about this ... Good night!

He slams the 'door'.

THE MAN: Phew! He can get nasty, can't he now? That was the chief engineer in my ministry. He says he wants his share. [*Laughs.*] Can you imagine that? His share? I work my arse off, and he wants his share. He's not getting a cent more from me. Not this time. All these people, you know, I have made them rich. Not this time. I use my brains, you know, I do all the leg work, and all they ever want is to share. I gave him twenty thousand rands, and that's it. That's enough for the part of the work that he did. And that applies to the others as well. The Director of Public Works and the Director of the Department of Tenders, I paid them twenty thousand rands each. I am being fair here. But do they accept it? No! They want us to get equal shares of the four million rands. And what did they do to deserve it?

Let me tell you exactly what happened, and I am sure you'll agree with me here that I have been fair. I always play fair, you know, and I want you to be fair to me as well. This is what happened. The government got funding, eh, from some international organisation — I won't tell you which one — for the resurfacing of the old road that links the capital to one of the district towns. You know, the road was in a mess with potholes. In fact potholes is an understatement. Some of them were real deep gullies — dongas so to say. That's why it took so long to resurface. They had to scrape off the old surface and reconstruct the whole thing. Anyway the job was advertised as usual. We are always fair, you know, we want to give every company the opportunity to bid for the job.

There is a humble knock at the 'door'.

THE MAN: Who can that be? Honey, I hope it's you.

He opens the 'door'.

THE MAN: Oh, it's you, Mr Director of the Department of Tenders ... Now, what can I do for you? ... Ah, so you have received the twenty thou that I left for you in your pigeon hole at the club. That's very nice, isn't it. It's always nice when a nice amount like that just drops in your lap so unexpectedly ... What? You are not satisfied with the amount? ... Now, tell me my friend, why are you not satisfied with the amount? ... I think it is enough for the role you played. I mean, what hard work did you do really, to deserve more than twenty thou? What risks did you take? I mean all you did was to make sure that we select the tender ... Who told you that I received four million rands for the job? Rumors! Mere rumours! I received some money, yes, but you are aware that there are many of us involved in this business. I had to pay quite a few people, and I have to share with my minister as ... Let's not be greedy, sir. We can't get rich on one day. You can see that our country is developing at a very fast rate. This of course means that there will be a lot of construction happening, and as usual we shall give the tenders to those companies that are willing to give us a good kickback ... So you see it is not fair for you to demand a big amount just for this one contract for resurfacing the road ... Well, it is true that we chose the particular tender because the contractor promised to pay us a ten percent kickback if we gave him the contract instead of his competitors ... Yes, the whole job was tendered for forty million ... Yes of course, ten percent of forty million is four million ... But I tell you the truth when I say that the contractor turned against his word. He paid only a fraction of what he promised, and there is nothing we can do about it. [*Laughs.*] We can't take him to the police now, can we? ... I am glad you understand ... [*Conspiratorially.*] Now, listen, we'll surely work something out that will make it worth our while. Don't you worry, we still have a lot that we'll do. Let's not kill the goose just yet. We are going to get lots and lots of golden eggs from it. Greed, and wanting to be a millionaire in one day, will surely kill the goose ... Good night, and do have the sweetest of dreams.

He closes the 'door'.

THE MAN: What a nerve! This is not my night at all. Not my day either. Nothing seems to go right. First the airplane, then I come home and my wife is nowhere to be seen, and then I am invaded by the Chief Engineer who is in fact my junior in the ministry, and now a confrontation with the Director of the Department of Tenders. Well, at least he is a gentleman, unlike the rude Chief Engineer who thinks I will shake out of my pants and share my money with him. He is a gentleman, this one. After all there is nothing that the Department of Tenders does except to implement our decisions and facilitate the choice of the tenders we want. For instance take the road that has caused all this quarrel. Yes, the road. It was advertised. Both international and local companies tendered for it. Fair is fair. Then we, that is the Chief Engineer, the Director of Public Works, and myself, examine the tenders because we have the expertise in these matters. The Director of the Department of Tenders has no expertise in road construction, has he now? We only put him in the deal because he was beginning to raise such stupid questions as why didn't we choose the lowest tender, which was from a local company to boot. He was beginning to make too much noise about that, so we had to let him into the secret that we chose the forty million rand tender, even though it was the highest, because the contractor promised us a ten percent kickback. Well, I didn't say ten percent to them. I am not that stupid. I only said that he promised to pay us a little something. They only took it for granted that it was going to be ten percent because that's the standard rate for kickbacks in this country. So, you see that the involvement of the Director of the Department of Tenders was very minimal in this matter? He'll get nothing more than the money that I gave him.

The following is said to the rhythm of guitar and drums.

THE MAN: I hear whispers and your snide remarks. Who of you here can claim to have clean hands? Now, you tell me! Did you buy those BMs and Benzes that you drive with your meagre salaries? I am no different from any one of you. The word that we use here at home is that we eat! Our culture today is that of eating. Everybody eats. From the most junior civil servant to the senior most guy. The shortest road to becoming a millionaire is to join the civil service or one of the parastatals. [*Sings.*] Join the civil service and be a millionaire.

The telephone rings. He answers.

THE MAN: Hello ... Oh, it's you again, Jane ... No, she is not back yet ... I am getting worried, Jane. I should be going out to look for her, but where do I begin? You are the only friend she has. If she is not with you I have no way of knowing where she can be ... And it's getting real late now ... Oh, Jane, you have no idea what I have been through just this past hour. I have been through hell ... No, no, just people invading my privacy. Selfish colleagues demanding this or that. Greedy workmates threatening me with all sorts of ridiculous violence against my person. You know, when you are successful people always want to destroy you ... My God! What could have happened to my wife? ... Joe is not back either? ... Listen, Jane, I'll call you back. I'll keep you abreast of the developments ... You keep well now, and don't worry your pretty little head too much ... We can only go to the police as a last resort ... Bye now.

He puts the receiver down.

THE MAN: She's a fine lady, this Jane. Sometimes I envy Joe. Not that I am not satisfied with my lot, you understand? I am quite happy. Happily married, with two or three mistresses on the side, as is the custom with us. I have a good family life, which was only marred by the fact that for all the years of our marriage we were not blessed with children. Without children our marriage was rather empty. For instance, who would inherit my millions when I die? But then we loved each other a lot, and kept on trying. We even went to *inyangas* and *sangomas* all over Southern Africa. We never gave up hope. And presto! Eight months ago she discovered that she was pregnant. Perfect happiness. Although of course she is having a difficult pregnancy. She'll pull through though. She is a very strong woman. In a month's time we are going to have our baby boy. With modern technology we know already that it is a boy. A boy who will inherit all the riches that I have accumulated throughout my years in the civil service.

So you see, I have fulfilment in my life. And I wish Jane had the same kind of fulfilment. But then she got married to a very stupid guy, who goes by the false adage that honesty is the best policy. Don't get me wrong. I don't hate Joe. I merely despise his principles. Joe has been a friend of mine since we were kids. We practically grew up together. We went to the same high school. Then to university. After university we both joined the civil service. I became a purchasing officer at the Ministry of Health, he became a billing clerk in one of our biggest parastatals, the Power Supply Corporation.

Both Joe and I started work as starry-eyed youths. We were straight from school, mind you, with all the idealistic enthusiasm of building the nation, and of working hard for the development of our country. Like all idealistic youths we were prepared to sacrifice for our country, and we despised those who left to work in foreign countries in search of greener pastures. Our driving force was the spirit of patriotism that we had cultivated in ourselves through political activism at university. We looked at life through rose-coloured glasses. By God! We were going to build this country!

Purchasing officer? That's a junior job. I come back from the university with a degree, and they make me a purchasing officer. Better positions, or what I thought were better positions, were occupied by old unschooled civil servants who looked at us young graduates with suspicious eyes. We were a threat, so they created a closed shop. I took the job of a guy who had been promoted to a better position, but to my surprise this guy was hankering after his old job. He missed being purchasing officer, and he envied me, his junior. At first I could not understand why. Very soon it dawned on me why mine was a prime job that everyone wanted. [*Smiles at the fond memory.*] You see, reps came selling all sorts of things. Drugs mostly. And hospital equipment. Different companies competing to sell stuff to the ministry, and I was the purchasing officer. This is what used to happen: a rep would invite me for a drink at one of the posh bars in town, and there he would lay his cards down. I buy the equipment or drugs from his company, and I get a slice of the cake. At first I refused. I was a scared greenhorn. But friends advised me, 'Don't be stupid. People are eating out there. Everyone has his or her hand in some till. The big ones, our leaders, are eating, but they expect us to sacrifice and work for our country out of some illusory concept called patriotism, whilst they are busy looting the coffers of the state!' Man, these were words of wisdom. I looked at my salary. What a pittance! I looked at what these reps were offering me. I saw the light! The scam was very simple. An item, say a new stethoscope, would cost five thousand rands, but then it would be invoiced by the rep, using his own invoice forms from the company, for fifty thousand. The government would pay, and the rep and I would share the forty five thou. We had our own secret accounts through which these government cheques were deposited. It was a piece of cake really. You see, no one ever checks, and if they check at all no one really knows how much a stethoscope should cost.

Well, don't pretend you are surprised at all this. We are not at all peculiar in this sort of thing. You remember in America a few years back, during the days of Mr Reagan's sleaze factory, the big guns at the Pentagon would buy a single nail for a thousand dollars. Why do you expect us to be different when our masters in the First World are prone to the same habit of eating? Well, anyway, that's how I started to move up the ladder of success. In no time I had built myself a house, I had bought myself a luxury car, I was taking overseas holidays, and I was generally living it up. And you know what? Nobody asked me a thing. Nobody questioned, even in secret corridors behind my back, how I could do all these things with my miserable government salary. People seemed to take it as a normal thing for a purchasing officer in a government ministry to be a very wealthy man indeed.

You know what, there is something about human beings. The more money you get, the greedier you become. I wanted to be a millionaire within a very short space of time. I got into prohibited drugs. I made connections. My P.S. too was a smart fellow who was on to mandrax. Selling them, that is. So we had our shit together, man. But you know, things like mandrax I don't like touching them. Even the P.S. was stupid to get into such things when he had all the opportunity to get lots and lots of money the easy way from government purchases and government contracts. So I decided to keep clear of his drug deals, and concentrated on making a living the old-fashioned way, by inflating invoices and taking kickbacks from companies which sold the ministry all sorts of things. Sometimes things which were not essential, or even necessary, for the hospitals I would buy just so as to get my commission.

Then one day things went wrong. The new Deputy Principal Secretary was a very vigilant man. He had just been promoted to that post. He was the type I despise, the Joe-type, an honest man, a man on a crusade, a man who thought he could single-handedly wipe out what misguided people like him call corruption. One day he calls me to his office.

'I was looking at these invoices, Mr Modise,' he says.

'A very good job, sir, if I may say so myself,' I innocently respond.

'How is it possible, Mr Modise?'

'How is what possible, sir?'

'I see here you bought bedpans. Fifty bedpans.'

'Oh, yes, the bedpans. For the hospital in Leribe. They need fifty more bedpans because of the extension to the hospital. They are now able to admit more patients. And it really is a good thing, sir, now that the hospital has been extended. If only the same ...'

'All right, Mr Modise, I understand all that. I have no problem with the number of bedpans that were ordered.'

'I am glad to hear that, sir. It was their own requisition. And you know, sir, they are very good bedpans too. Good-bye, sir.'

'I am not through yet, Mr Modise. Come back. I have a problem with the figures on these invoices.'

Aha! I smelt a rat. What is he trying to tell me? Is the bastard trying to be smart or what? A problem with the figures?

'Yes, Mr Modise, we have been billed fifty thousand rands for fifty bedpans.'

'Well, I don't see anything wrong with that, sir.'

'What kind of bedpans, Mr Modise, would cost one thousand rand each?'

'Well, sir ... '

'A chamber pot for a thousand rands, Mr Modise!'

'This is not just a simple chamber pot. It is specially designed for use in a hospital. And you know that hospital equipment is generally expensive, sir.'

He laughs. He laughs for a long time. I am beginning to seethe with anger. What the shit is he laughing at? Look at his big ugly teeth. Look at his rough stupid face, a face that has been scarred by poverty. Smell the fumes of poverty emitted by his unwashed mouth.

'You know, Mr Modise, I phoned the company. [O-o.] The managing director is just as surprised. He was shocked in fact. No bedpan in the history of his company has ever cost that much. You are in this scam with his rep. The rep is surely going to lose his job, and I'll be damned if I don't see to it that you lose yours as well. It is people like you who have given this government a bad name. It is people like you who have made the Third World the laughing stock of the so-called developed world.'

Oh, so now he wants to save the whole Third World from the likes of me. That's it. I am in shit street. I am going to lose my job. What the hell shall I do? I have some money in the bank, of course. But it's not that much. I spent it all on various luxuries. Go and see my sumptuous, nay palatial, house. Walk inside and admire my furniture. Relax in my jacuzzi if you like. I mean, when you don't expect a thing like this will happen to you so soon, you don't save. As the money comes you spend it.

You know that tomorrow you'll make some more. Then, only then, will you invest in some kind of business. So, you see, I had not yet started investing my money. I was still on a spending spree. And now all of a sudden the feast is over! All the same I consoled myself that I had eaten!

A month passed. Nothing happened. To me, that is. Guess what I received the following month. Come on, guess. A letter of dismissal? [*He laughs for a long time. He really is enjoying himself.*] I received a promotion! I was made Deputy Principal Secretary, in place of that nosey D.P.S. who thought he could get me expelled from the civil service. He, instead, was transferred to some other department where he would be harmless. You see, the big bosses, the ministers and all those closer to God, saw that he was a dangerous man who was bent on exposing so-called corruption. If he started by exposing me, his junior, he would surely end up exposing them as well. He was dangerous. So they transferred him. He became the Director of the Department of Manpower Development — a very harmless post for a man like him. Or so they thought, for I have no doubt that when he got there he started rooting out all those who gave scholarships to their lovers and relatives, or those who sold them to prospective candidates. Well, I was promoted. I took his place. You see, in the government here, when they discover your corruption they promote you. There are two reasons for that. The first one is that they want to shut your mouth so that you won't reveal what you know which may expose some of the top dogs in the government. The next reason, which is more important, is that they appreciate your brains, and they want to bring you closer to them up there, so that they may benefit from your expertise in corruption — learn new techniques from you. You see, in many cases ministers have a problem, especially when they are new. They are just laymen. Remember that they sometimes come as country bumpkins who know nothing about these things. Bumpkins who are hungry, but lack sophistication. They want to eat, but are ignorant of the methods. They need top civil servants like us to help them to eat. We are indispensable.

Well, I became D.P.S. It was only a matter of months. Perhaps a year. They made me Principal Secretary, first of Health, then I moved from ministry to ministry, until I ended up at this most lucrative ministry, where I deal with big multi-million rand government projects. And in the meantime what happened to Joe? Wait, let me go to the kitchen and have a drink of water. I'll come back and tell you about the fate of Joe at the Power Supply Corporation.

He goes out. Guitar and drums for a few beats.

Scene Three

THE MAN enters driving a steering wheel. He has changed some of his clothes to give himself a different identity. Not much change though, for he is still THE MAN. For instance, if he was wearing a jacket in the previous scenes, he is not wearing it in this scene — or vice versa.

THE MAN: Vrooom ... vro-o-o-o-oom! Po-o-o-op! Vroo-o-o-oom!

He sits on one of the chairs, directly facing the audience. He drives for some time, changing gears when necessary.

THE MAN [*while driving*]: Vroo-o-oom! Well, I promised I would tell you what was happening to Joe. While I was busy oiling myself with the fat of the land, enjoying the fruits of independence, what our East African brothers call *matundu uhuru*, Joe was a hardworking clerk at the Power Supply Corporation. You know, the organisation that lights up our lives. Joe has always been hardworking. So, through a combination of sweat and tears he diligently worked himself up — climbing the rungs of the corporate ladder very rapidly. Until he became counterpart to the Managing Director. That's the highest you can get. The M.D. was a European guy who had followed his country's aid which was funding the Power Supply Corporation.

So, like I said, Joe was the counterpart. He was being trained to take over one day as Managing Director. I was so happy for him, for I knew that he was going to eat. As an M.D. of a big corporation like that you can eat left, right, and centre. So what happens to Joe? Let me tell you, and you will see why I am so disgusted with him. Perhaps I will tell the story best if I become Joe — just for a short while though for I wouldn't want to be an idiot for a long time. Okay, I am Joe now. I am driving to work. It is in the morning. The Maseru traffic is rather slow in the morning. Goddamn it! That taxi driver nearly hit me. Taxi drivers are the same all over. They drive shit and have no consideration for other road users. Taxi drivers are number one in rotten driving. They are followed by drivers of government vehicles. Then truck drivers of all types.

Suddenly he swerves, and has to stop the car.

THE MAN: What the hell! A ditch! They have dug a ditch right in the middle of the road. They always do this. Trenches! You can't just drive from point A to point B anywhere in this city without coming across a deadly trench, with inadequate or no warning signs to boot.

He starts the car again and drives on.

THE MAN: These are death traps. I think this is somebody's plan up there, somebody who is trying take a short cut in decreasing the escalating population of this country. Somebody has seen that family planning and child spacing programmes do not seem to work, the population is growing at an alarming rate. So the best solution is to make these death traps, with the hope that they will take the lives of quite a few people.

My God! This traffic is so slow moving. There is no doubt that I'll be late at the office today. And that's going to be a very bad example. I am a stickler for punctuality. That's one thing they hate about me at the office. I insist that everyone should be at work at eight sharp, ever since I became counterpart to the Managing Director.

Another thing, of course, which contributes to traffic congestion in the mornings and afternoons, besides the deathtraps that they are always digging all over the road, is that Maseru is really a one street town. That's due to bad British planning — or non-planning. Our colonial masters had no intention of making us a beautiful city we could all be proud of. It seems it was meant to be a temporary administrative camp, with no potential for growth. And then we took over after independence and reinforced the bad planning. We made it worse, in fact. Have you seen how haphazard this city is? I am talking now of new places, places which emerged long after the colonial officer had packed his bags and had been replaced by neo-colonial officers from various countries of the world. At the time when we have all sorts of international experts, and when we have our own people who have come back from abroad with Masters degrees and PhDs in urban planning, in all fields of architecture, you get newly created slums such as the one you find at Lithoteng Ha Seoli. You know the place I am talking about, where people have just put up houses anywhere and anyhow, to the extent that some households, some sites and plots, have no access to any street whatsoever. Those who live in those houses have to fly to get to their houses. We get places where we have a mess of residential houses and factories in the same area. Yet in our civil service we have all these highly trained experts. We have our own people as chief engineers, town planners, and what have you. What the hell are they doing there? I'll tell you what they are doing. They are eating. Yes, that's our national pastime, eating! We say the spout of the kettle is facing us, so let us eat! Our engineers, our town planners, our bureaucrats of all sorts, have gained expertise in a new field altogether, that of eating! Everyone is eating left and right. Yes, the mother of all eating is happening right here in this country at this moment in history.

He stops his monologue for a while and drives the car.

THE MAN: Vrooo-o-o-oom ... vro-o-o-oom! [*Checking his watch.*] My God, it is almost nine o'clock. I am one hour late already, and all because of this traffic. Believe it or not, I left home at seven, thinking that at eight I would be at work, since I live only a few kilometers away from the office.

He gets out of the car and walks into his office.

THE MAN: Hi, Nthabi! ... Oh, the Managing Director wants to see me? Do you know what about? ... Can it be that it's because I am late? After all he comes late too sometimes ... Well, anyway, let me see him right away.

He is now with the Managing Director.

THE MAN: Good morning, sir. I am late because ... Oh, that's not what you want to talk about. What is it then? ... Oh, my requisition for new furniture in my house? Yes, I have made that requisition because now that I am Deputy Managing Director and your counterpart I have moved to the new house that was occupied by the previous deputy. But it has no furniture, since he took all the corporation's furniture with him when he left ... But sir, what do you mean I can't get new furniture? What am I supposed to use? ... That's grossly unfair, sir. I think I deserve to have furniture in the company house, like all the other senior staff ... Look, the Senior Engineer for instance, who is my junior but is white and is your compatriot, has posh furniture in his house, the Accountant, who is also your compatriot, has posh furniture. All the white employees have posh furniture in their houses, purchased by the corporation. They have better houses too than all the local senior staff. Why can't I have decent furniture? ... Why do you accuse me of being a troublemaker? And why do you want us to be fighting all the time? Yesterday you accused me of creating bad working relations with my fellow workers, only because I insisted that a technician who was using a company car as a taxi must be punished. ... And all because you do not want me to clean up the corruption here. What I want to know is, what are you getting out of this rotten situation? Why do you want to maintain it? ... No, no, I am not insulting you ... I am not even insinuating that you are involved in corruption ... Well, you don't even have to boast to me about that, for I know very well that the money that established this corporation is from your country, and that you were sent here by your government as an expert ... [*He laughs.*] Expert! I mean were you a local you would only be a technician really — with your diploma from a technical school! We do have people here with senior degrees in your field, you know. But then because you are from overseas, and your country is donating the money, you are an expert! ... Please don't get angry ... No, no, no, don't get angry. I am only stating facts ... What? You say we are beggars and we have no right to complain, that you know best what is good for us, especially if it is your country's money that we are talking about here ... Is that why you treat everyone with so much disrespect, Mr Expert? ... Remember last week we had such a big dispute that we had to take it to a Cabinet minister. I had hoped that the Honourable Minister, as Chairman of the Board of the Power Supply Corporation would settle the dispute one way or the other, and would bring us together so that we could work in peace for the betterment of this corporation. But, no! you had to bully the Honourable Minister. You even said 'Rubbish!' to him when he was trying to make a suggestion, trying solve the problem. Then finally you threatened to withdraw your country's aid from Lesotho if I was not sacked from this corporation ... Oh, so you still insist that I must be fired ... You say I have caused a lot of trouble since joining this corporation. But I am only trying to do my job ... Take what happened last month, for instance ... Yes, the scandal of the meter readers ... You know the facts of this case very well, but I will repeat them to you for the last time ... A lot of important people in this city bribed meter readers to make electricity meters reverse instead of going forward in relation to the consumption of electricity. Important people were involved! Rich people! Directors, lawyers, big businessmen, even ministers! ... This had been going on for a long time. But when I took over as your Deputy M.D. I became suspicious when some real big businesses were having electricity bills of one rand a month. I then asked that a random list of our customers should be compiled, and their bills should be investigated. I tell you, ninety percent of them were found to be involved in this scam ... I did not do that! Somebody from this office leaked an internal document containing the random list, and it was all over in the streets! Suddenly there was a contract on my head ... And from you, Mr Expert, and from my minister I expected support ... Instead I am threatened with sacking. Even though I was trying to root out corruption and make this corporation run at a profit. Look, right now the people who were discovered to be involved in the scam are paying back thousands of rands, and the corporation is really getting its money back ... Are you not happy? ... Then you said I should take action against the meter readers. All of a sudden I was the one who had to fire the meter readers ... You knew very well that I could not fire them because they were members of the Youth League of the ruling party ... Instead I was summoned, actually frogmarched, to the party office, where the Honourable Minister instructed me to apologise to the meter readers, and to you Mr Expert, and to all the inconvenienced customers ... Now, let me tell you, Mr Expert, I refuse to apologise! [*Almost hysterically.*] I refuse! I refuse! I refuse to apologise!

The guitar and drums join in.

THE MAN [*screaming*]: I refuse, Mr Expert! I refuse! I refuse!

He grabs his steering wheel, and runs out screaming. The music continues for a few minutes.

Scene Four

THE MAN *enters, with his briefcase. He is now himself, not Joe.*

THE MAN: Well, that's what happened to Joe. You see, he had all the opportunities to make it big there, but he messed things up. He tried to be a goody-goody who wanted to stop everyone from eating. At the same time he was a thorn in the asshole of the expert managing director. Then one day, just in front of the LNDC Centre there, some crooks tried to hijack the MD's car at gunpoint. A shot was fired, which missed him or perhaps grazed him. He accused Joe of being responsible for that. I mean Joe would not do a thing like that, but the MD said Joe must have hired the crooks to kill him and steal his car. So he said it was no longer safe for him in Lesotho. He withdrew his country's aid and left the country.

He laughs for a long time.

THE MAN: The Honourable Minister was very angry, of course. Everyone hated Joe. But at that stage there was a crisis at the Power Supply Corporation. They could not expel Joe, for he was the only one who knew the job of running the corporation. So they made him acting MD. Now if he was smart that should have been his opportunity to make amends and prove himself to his minister and colleagues. He should have shown everybody that he was capable of eating as well as any man. But no! His stupidity triumphs again. Oh, I have never seen anyone so stupid in my life. That's when I finally lost all respect for Joe. He is beyond redemption.

There was a contract for a multimillion rand project that had to be carried out for his Power Supply Corporation. Joe could have made a killing there. Well, contractors tendered for the job. Joe employed independent consultants to evaluate the tenders. They chose a Swedish company which had its own finance at three percent. It had tendered for twenty million rands and, like I say, was financing the project itself at only three percent interest. The Honourable Minister and his Permanent Secretary were very angry with him. They had wanted him to take a forty-six million rand tender instead. The forty million would have gone to the contractor, and the six million divided among the three of them. Joe would have been a millionaire now. But no, he said no. He wanted the Swedish company that was not going to pay any kickbacks to anyone. Well, the big guns had had enough of Joe and his holier-than-thou attitude towards our noble tradition of eating. They fired him. After being kicked out from Power Supply Joe moved from job to job. Every time he gets a good job with a lot of prospects for eating, he tries to be honest. So they kick him out. I have told him, 'Wake up, Joe! Wake up!' But Joe will never wake up. Right now he is unemployed.

He sits down and seems to be deep in thought. The band plays softly. After a while he worriedly paces the floor. He is troubled.

THE MAN: Do you think I should call the police? Maybe? Mm? Maybe something has happened to her. I mean, this has never happened before. She has never just disappeared like a fart in the air. Sometimes she goes out for a drink with the girls. Well, she used to. But now that she is pregnant she has stopped drinking altogether. That's why I don't understand her disappearance. No note. No word. Nothing. It is past midnight. No word. Maybe I should call the police. But no, let me wait a bit. What if she's gone away with somebody. An old flame perhaps. After all she did not expect me back from Jo'burg for the next two days or so. I won't call the police yet. I don't want to cause an unnecessary scandal. I am a very important man in the community, you know. I wouldn't like the police to pry into my private family affairs.

There is a loud knock. At the same time the music of the band stops.

THE MAN: What now? Honey, I hope it's you.

He opens the door.

THE MAN: Good gracious, what brings you here at this time? ...
They what? ... They plan to do something real terrible to me?
But why? ... Why should they hate me when all I did was just to
eat? Is it because I do it better than everyone else, with a lot of
finesse and sophistication? Do they hate me because I am a big
time eater, and I am in the big league of the eating game, while
they remain small time eaters in the little leagues? I have devised
new methods of eating, while they remain with their crude
outdated methods ... But I am glad that you came to warn me ...
You have always been a true friend. That is why I am very keen
to teach you the very modern methods of eating ... You will get
very far I tell you. At the moment you are only a messenger in
my office, but you are doing a very good job spying for me on
what my colleagues are doing, or saying, or planning against
me. A very good job indeed ... And I do pay you well, don't I.
And if you sharpen your skills of eating, you will end up a very
rich man indeed, for you'll have been trained by the best ...
What do you mean mere messengers have no opportunities for
eating? ... [*Laughs.*] You are mistaken, my friend. There is no
work situation in the government service that will not avail a
creative worker the opportunity to eat. Any job can be used for
eating. You just need to be creative, that's all ... Let me tell you,
only a few days ago I was pitying the young women and men
who work until late at the border posts ... Yes, I am talking
about the people at customs. I shouldn't have pitied them. A
lot of them, the wiser ones that is, enjoy it there. I learnt this
when I bought a fridge at Ladybrand in South Africa. They don't
charge tax there because it's going to Lesotho and sales tax will
be charged at the border post by Lesotho customs officers. But
you know what? I didn't pay any sales tax for that fridge. Well,
I paid some little money. The sales tax I was supposed to pay
was four hundred rands, but I paid only one hundred to the
customs woman at the border post. She pocketed the money,
and let me pass. I saved three hundred rands. You can imagine
how many people cross at that border post each day, with all
sorts of goods, and how many hundred rands that woman got

in that one day. Not less than a thousand, I tell you. So you see, she has mastered the art of eating in her job. She has turned a lousy boring job into a highly profitable business where she nets not less than a thousand rands each day ... So don't be dumb, my friend. Even though you are a mere messenger, you can devise ways and means of eating ... I will have sessions with you, where I will give you thorough training in the art of eating. But for now I want you to tell me exactly what they are planning against me ... Oh, so it is the Chief Engineer, the Director of Works, the Director of the Hydro-Electric Scheme, and the Director of the Tender Board. I see, I see ... Oh, so they are in a meeting right now plotting my downfall? The snakes! What is their problem? ... They say I left them out of some important deals, that I have been eating alone and not sharing with them. Do they ever share with me? Don't they ever make their own private deals without letting me into the secret? Take the Director of the Hydro-Electric Scheme, for instance. Is he not a multi-millionaire twice over? Did I ever question him why he did not share with me? ... Anyway I am glad you came to warn me. Go back there and listen some more, and come back and tell me ... What, you want me to pay you more money? ... You know, I have always trusted you, and I know that you have been loyal to me, but now what do you mean when you say you want me to pay you more money? ... That's greed, my friend ... Let me tell you, if you want to be successful in this game you must not be greedy ... You must be grateful for the things I am doing for you ... Like teaching you the most modern methods of eating ... In fact even now I am planning to recommend you for promotion ... You will be a clerk one day ... [*Smiles.*] Eh, what do you think of that? A clerk! Eat! Eat! Clerks eat. Eh, my friend. You will eat. Now, go away, my friend, eh. Let's not hear any more talk of wanting to be paid more money.

He opens the door.

THE MAN: Now, goodbye. [*Shouting after him.*] Do come back and give me more information about those snakes!

He closes the door.

THE MAN: The twerp! Now he says he wants more money! Why are people so greedy? Why are they never satisfied with what they have? As for promotion, he'll never see it. I do not have the time to break in a new messenger to spy for me. As for those snakes who are plotting against me, they don't know what they are up against! It is the same greed that I am talking about. And the Director of the Hydro-Electric Scheme has a nerve, joining those snakes against me. I have been eating with him all the time. He has even eaten more than me, and I have saved his skin a few times too! Only recently a scandal nearly broke out about his dealings with a French company. You know the French. Oh ho! They are great in the business of eating. They are not afraid to pay real big moneys to get contracts. So what happened here was that this fool flew to France to clinch a deal with a French company which had completed a job on some aspects of the Hydro-Electric Scheme. And you know what he did with his French accomplices? They inflated the claim, a very stupid thing to do. You know that when a claim is inflated like that it goes for arbitration, and any crookedness will be discovered there. The smart thing to do is to inflate the initial price, arrange with the contractor to charge more than the job is really worth at the tender stage, and then share the excess with the contractor. I mean, this guy knew that very well, for he had done it many times before. He is already a multi-millionaire who does all his shopping, even for groceries, in London and New York. It was just greed which made him inflate the claim. Moreover he left his deputy out of the deal, so the deputy was very angry, and was keen that action be taken against him. He was canvassing everybody, including the Honourable Minister, to fire the bastard. I saved him. Fortunately at that time a relative of the minister — I think it was a cousin of his grandmother's uncle — died. So I advised the guy to contribute two thousand rands towards the funeral expenses. The minister was quite happy and the guy was not

27

fired. And here he is, turning against me, plotting with snakes against me.

He is very angry now, so angry that he can't speak.

THE MAN: Well, the Chief Engineer and the Director of Tenders, you have seen them here already. You heard their problem. The Director of Works's problem is the same one. The road. They all want a share from the proceeds of the road. That's one road that has given me problems, not only with my colleagues, but with the contractor as well. The road that leads to the southern towns. I hate that road! Oh, how I hate that road! It is costing me more than it is really worth. It was one of the smallest contracts that I have handled, a mere forty million rand, and I got a mere four million. I have handled bigger contracts, costing hundreds and hundreds of millions. And I have eaten from all these. They never caused me any problem. But this measly contract is causing me so much trouble. You see, this is what is happening here: I told you how the contractor paid me four million rands to get the contract. He resurfaced the road, but did a very cheap job, very shoddy, with a very very thin layer of tar. After a month there were potholes all over the road. And then it rained. The potholes became worse. People were beginning to ask questions, 'This road is only a month old. How come it is like this? Full of all these potholes?' It was embarrassing the government, particularly because the money for resurfacing the road came from one of our friendly overseas donors. I went to the contractor. I told him it was bad faith the way he did the job. He became arrogant because he knew I could not do anything about it. He shouted at me, 'We paid you some of the money we could have used to make a better road. We deposited millions in your Swiss bank account. With what do you expect us to make you a better road?' My God! What was I going to do? The contractor with whom we were in this was turning against me. Meanwhile the potholes were getting bigger. So I went to my friend the Director of Public Works and asked him to use his department to patch up some of the potholes. He knew my problems. He knew that I had received some money from the original contractor, and he demanded some of it. I said, 'Okay, man, I'll give you some of the money.' So he sent his orange-overalled brigade to patch the potholes. But it is proving to be an impossible job. You patch here, then the next day there is a big hole just next to that. The problem is still not solved. There are dongas in the road. And the Director of Works has the nerve to demand to be paid! I will surely sort this business out somehow.

He takes a long look at the audience.

THE MAN [*frantically*]: Come on! Don't be so judgemental against me. Don't look at me as if I have killed someone! I have told you already that I am not doing anything that others are not doing. There is no need to hide it any more. We must be open about it, for we are doing it in the interests of this country. For the development and economic growth of our beloved country. All countries in the world will do anything to protect their interests. That is how the world works. The U.S., that citadel of democracy, will commit acts of terrorism by mining the harbours of Nicaragua, or will assassinate foreign leaders through their CIA. What I am trying to say here is that there is no country in the world that will not engage in underhand activities in order to protect the interests of that country. Why do you expect Lesotho to be different? It is in the interests of this country that you should have some millionaires like us, so that you can proudly point us out to the world and say, 'We too, in our country, we are developing, we have our own millionaires.' The poor will always be with us, for it is quite easy to be poor. To accumulate wealth, on the other hand, is an achievement which requires hard work and brain power, and deserves praise instead of condemnation. So be proud of us millionaires! Shower us with praise! Love and kiss us all the time you meet us in the streets! For we are the glory of your country!

The action is becoming more frantic and pathetic.

THE MAN: Why should we be different? We are just as good as any country, so we are going to engage in filth like any other decent country in the world. All I am saying is that we now need to engage in these activities openly. For instance we have now started selling Lesotho passports on the international open market. That is good. We have an agent who is selling them for us. But we need to be more creative in the world of business, in our marketing efforts. We must start selling these passports in the supermarkets of Hong Kong and Taiwan. Just like the gossip tabloids and magazines. Housewives can go and shop for groceries, and buy a passport if they so wish. The price will also go down for we'll be making real bulk sales. The current price is rather steep for an ordinary Chinese housewife. Only a few can be sold at the current price but if you bring the price down and sell them at the supermarket you will sell a lot, and make more profit. The principle is: small profits, quick returns. It is an excellent idea, this selling of passports, thought out by a real genius. For a few dollars you get instant citizenship. It doesn't matter if you don't even know where Lesotho is on the map, you get an instant Lesotho passport. Now, I strongly advocate that we must go a step further. We must establish a new ministry. The Ministry for the Promotion of Drug Smugglers, Mafiosi, and Triad Gangs. I wouldn't mind if I were promoted to that ministry.

Even more frantic and pathetic.

THE MAN: Please don't look at me like that. Would you rather I remained poor like the rest of the population of this country? Would you rather I retire in utmost poverty? Did you hear what happened to Kaunda of Zambia? He ruled for all those years, but was stupid enough not to eat. The young fellas came and removed him from office through the ballot box. Now he's poor. He hasn't even got a house of his own. The ANC of South Africa had to donate a house to him in appreciation for his role in the struggle. Now the new government is not even giving him a pension. All the other African heads of state are looking at things like these, and if they don't want what happened to Kaunda to happen to them, they will accumulate wealth in Swiss banks as fast as they can, so that when a democratic order comes they will have something to retire on. The Kaunda story has taught them a lesson. Is he now going to eat his honesty? This lesson, of course, also applies to us top civil servants. What guarantees are there that new governments will continue to pay us our pensions when we retire? So we must eat now while we can!

So please, don't give me that look of disgust. Do you know the consequences of poverty? Poverty is a sin, punishable by death. Would you rather I joined the ranks of the poor, like Joe, in spite of my talents? I am scared of poverty! Have you seen how this country treats the poor? You want me to give you an example of what I am talking about? Go to Queen Victoria Hospital right now. You can drive in and out of the hospital yard without anyone bothering you. But walk out on foot through the hospital gate, and a whole battalion of security people will search your bag — especially if you are a woman — and frisk you like a criminal. Why, because you are poor, and cannot afford to drive a car. You see, we operate under the staunch principle that if you drive a car, you cannot be a thief. But if you walk, you are poor, then surely you are a criminal! You are likely to steal spoons, forks, and penicillin from the hospital. Yes, the poor are criminals. Poverty is a crime!

On my way from the airport last evening there was a road block. They stopped all the vehicles. From the drivers they asked for drivers' licences, and let them pass. But buses, no way! Everyone had to climb down. Luggage and handbags were thoroughly searched. Because the police also know that poverty is a crime. It is our tradition. Even during the old days when there were tax and radio licence raids, these would only happen in the areas where the poor people lived, never in your glittering suburbs.

I tell you, I refuse to be poor! I refuse! If this whole thing explodes in my face, and I am kicked out of my job, I am well protected from poverty. I have cushioned my nest very well, with wise investments. For instance I bought all the houses that were built by the Housing Corporation — built to relieve the housing shortage. I bought them all, and am renting them out at very high rent. A lot of white people are coming into the country bringing aid. I rent to them. Not to local blacks. They couldn't afford it anyway. Or would not pay rent timeously. It's easier to deal with white people. That's why even when I go to a place where I need service I go straight to a white person, even if there is a Mosotho offering the same service. A Mosotho does not wish to see a fellow Mosotho succeed in life. He will put as many obstacles as he can before him. He will display arrogance. He will make you feel that he is doing you a favour by serving you in his business. He will display power. Anyway I am digressing. I was telling you about my investments. Have you seen my house? Well, you have only seen this room. I tell you this is the best house in this town. Maybe one day I'll take you on a tour. It has ten bedrooms, twelve bathrooms, and six guest toilets. It has a reception area that can comfortably seat two hundred people. It has three large swimming pools, one indoor, and two outdoor. There are three tennis courts. Every bedroom has its own jacuzzi. There are gyms and saunas. It has ten garages and fifteen servants' rooms. It is surrounded by a three meter wall.

Still frantic, almost hysterical.

THE MAN: I refuse to be poor, sir! I refuse! I refuse! No one wants to be poor. Even traffic cops don't want to be poor. This evening on my way from the airport I paid a bribe to a traffic cop. You know, they have this new toy now, the speed trap. So I was driving one-twenty and I thought I was within the legal speed limit. I was stopped and was told that in fact the speed limit in the highways of this country is eighty kilometers per hour. I had to pay, for I understand that the traffic cop must also eat.

The phone rings. He answers.

THE MAN: Hello, is that you, Jane? ... Hey, who is this now? ... What is that you say ... My wife? ... Yes, that is her name ... Yes ... And you say you are calling from the hospital in Morija? ... Oh, my God! Oh, my God! ... Will she live? ... What about the baby? ... He is dead! ... My baby boy is dead! [*He is screaming.*] Do you think she is going to live, my wife, do you think she is going to live? ... What happened? Please tell me the whole story ... Mh ... Oh ... Ah ... Okay, thank you. I will come right away ... I'll phone his wife, and we'll both come right away!

He puts down the receiver, lifts it up and phones again.

THE MAN: Hello, Jane ... I have bad news, Jane ... Jane, please be brave ... Oh, you have heard already? Oh, my God, what are you going to do, Jane? ... Well, what I hear is this, when I was busy negotiating deals in Johannesburg my wife got labour pains. She phoned Joe for help, since she had given day-off to all our servants - including our chauffeur ... I think you were out at the time ... So Joe rushed here and immediately drove her in one of my twelve cars to Queen Victoria Hospital ... Yes, I am sure they both knew what kind of a hospital Queen Victoria is, and that more often than not they don't even have the basic drugs there. But this was an emergency, so they could not go to our usual private hospital in Johannesburg. So they had no option but to drive to Queen Victoria Hospital. When they got there, they had a very rough ride at the gate ... You know, there is that big hole that was dug many months ago ... Yes, one of our famous trenches that are all over the roads throughout the city. The big hole at the gate which is now almost always filled with water, where you will find poor women bathing their babies ... Anyway my wife was badly shaken when the car fell into that ditch. Joe took her into the hospital, but the nurses laughed at her, shouting, 'When you are in trouble you come here for help. But you didn't attend our clinic here. You, better people, you go to private doctors and private clinics. What do you want here now? Bring her here.' But my wife, in spite of the pain, was angry at this kind of treatment. So even though the nurses were going to help her, after shouting at her, she asked Joe to take her to Morija instead, which is forty kilometers away ... I supposed Joe drove like a madman. Until they got to the dongas on my road ... Well, that road which has patches all over ... Then the car overturned, and Joe was killed instantly ... And my baby, who by then had fought his way out of his mother's womb without anyone's help, also died instantly ... My wife is in a very serious condition ... She may die ... Even if she lives she will be handicapped forever. She broke her spinal cord at the neck ... [*Crying.*] Oh, Jane, what are we going to do? ... Oh, that road, I hate that road! ... That road has given me so many problems, and now it has killed the people I love ... Jane, please, let us be brave. Let us not cry ... What are these problems that I say have been caused by the road? Never mind. You won't understand. Listen, Jane, I am coming over there right away, then we'll drive to Morija.

He puts the receiver down. He is confused. He is in a daze. Sad music from the guitar and the drums. Perhaps the music had started some time during the telephone conversation. Then suddenly there is a rude knock. In a confused state he opens the door.

THE MAN: Who? ... What? ... It's my loyal messenger. Have you brought me news about those snakes? You'll have to wait. I have to go to the hospital in Morija. My wife ... What do you mean I am going to nowhere? ... Hey, what's wrong with you? Have you come to attack me? ... Why? ... You have always been my loyal messenger, my loyal spy, my loyal friend. Now this is my hour of sorrow, and you come to my house to tell me that today I will vomit all the money that I have stolen from other people ... I see, you have now been bought by my enemies ... Please, please, I have to go. We'll discuss this some other time. My wife ...

Obviously the messenger has hit him hard with a fist in the stomach, and he falls down. The sound effects of the blow are created with the drum.

THE MAN: Oh! You dare raise your hand against me! You, a mere messenger, hitting your master! I will call the police! I will shoot you ... Where is my gun? ... Oh, please, let me go. My wife needs me ...

He tries to stand up, but is obviously pushed down by the messenger. He kneels on the floor.

THE MAN: Now listen, if it's money you want, I'll give you any amount ... Just let me go to my dying wife ... What do you mean I am a rotten piece of shit, and that one day the people shall rise and take vengeance on the likes of me? What people? The people are blind! The people don't see! Or if they see they have no power to act. The people don't have any leadership that will create a critical awareness in them, that will open their eyes. Whenever new leadership emerges, even if it begins as honest leadership, it is swallowed by the culture of eating, and becomes one with it ... Yes, there is talk of a new democratic order. But political parties canvassing for elections compete over which party has better criminals than others ... The people are doomed to ... [*An obvious kick, and a scream.*] Okay, okay, I admit. One day the people shall rise. The people have the capacity to rise! The people are not blind! They may seem to be docile now, but it will take a very small thing to spark action in them, and to arouse them to an anger that has not been seen before ... But please, let me go ... I am sure we can discuss the various capabilities of the people some other time ... Hey, who are you calling now? ... Do you mean you have recruited people to attack me? ...

He stands up.

THE MAN: Who are these people who are coming in now? ... Oh, it's you Mr Chief Engineer, and you Mr Director of Public Works, and you Mr Director of the Tender Board, and you Mr Director of the Hydro-Electric Scheme. [*Tries to smile at them.*] How very nice to see you. For a moment I thought this rogue of a messenger had invited his common friends, or what he calls the people, to beat me up ... Oh, you have also come to beat me up! [*Laughs nervously.*] Well, at least I'll be beaten up by people of my class — fellow millionaires! ... Just joking, my friends ... Listen, my friends, I have a big problem. My wife ...

Suddenly he is hit in the stomach.

THE MAN [*screaming*]: Oh, please, don't hit me so hard ... Please forgive me ... I will share with you all the money I have ...

Blows rain on different parts of his body. We see him cringing, grimacing, falling down, trying to stand up again, then falling, all the time screaming. The drums create the sound effects for each blow. The guitar joins in to create sounds of pain and confusion.

THE MAN [*screaming*]: Please forgive me, my friends. [*Blow.*] I am very sorry for what I did to you. [*Blow.*] I will never do it again. [*Blow.*] You can take everything I have!

He is down now and cannot stand up any more.

THE MAN: Do you hear what the messenger is saying, you my friends who are trying to kill me now? ... Did you hear him? He says even you, my friends, even you, your day will dawn. He is not on your side. He says he is going to whip up the emotions of the common people who will rise against you ... He says he will do it even if it takes him a hundred years ... So you can beat me up now, but our time will come too ...

He receives a last kick on the stomach which finally shuts him up. He groans, and his body jerks and twitches. He is vomiting. He gasps once or twice, then lies silent. Is he dead, perhaps? Music crescendos and stops as lights fade to dark.

You Fool,
How Can the Sky Fall?

"The sky is falling! The sky is falling!" So said Chicken Little.

You Fool, How Can the Sky Fall? opened at the Windybrow Centre for the Arts, Johannesburg, on 6 March 1995, with Gamakhulu Diniso as The President, Anton Dekker as The General, Themba Ndaba as The Minister of Culture, Theresa Iglich as The Minister of Health, Darrill Rosen as The Minister of Justice, Ernest Ndlovu as The Minister of Agriculture and Desmond Dube as The Young Man.

The play was directed by Peter Se-Puma.

Cast

THE GENERAL ... Middle-aged male soldier
THE PRESIDENT ... Elderly man, benevolent dictator
MINISTER OF CULTURE ... Youngish man
MINISTER OF HEALTH ... Older woman
MINISTER OF JUSTICE ... Middle-aged man
MINISTER OF AGRICULTURE ... Middle-aged man
YOUNG MAN ... Late teens to early twenties, a dandy

Scene One

Lights rise on the stage. Four figures are frozen in what looks very much like a pose in an Old Master painting. They are a unit, but are on different planes. The emphasis is on a little man, quite scrawny in fact, with a bony face and penetrating eyes. He is old and frail, and looks as if he might break at any time. He wears a tattered suit that has a sheen of filth, a yellowing shirt that was once white, and a twisted tie. On one of his legs his pants are rolled up to the knee, and the leg is wrapped in a filthy bandage. He has no shoes. We shall later learn that he is His Excellency THE PRESIDENT. The rest are shoeless members of his Cabinet. They are a motley group of two men and one woman, plunged into the deepest levels of gloom imaginable: a menagerie of shapes and sizes in tattered and filthy clothes. His Excellency THE PRESIDENT, however, sports a broad self-satisfied smile.

Somewhere on the floor the sun has drawn bars from an unseen window so that we get the sense that our characters are locked up in a dingy cell. The shape and position of the bars will change as the position of the sun changes on its journey across the sky. At night the bars disappear and a dull yellowish light illuminates the lives of our characters. The upstage planes remain very dim throughout the play. These planes are known as the Shadows. If you are not using a proscenium you designate the weakest area/plane on your thrust, arena and so on as the Shadows. The Shadows are not totally dark. For instance when our characters are in the Shadows we can see them, and can sometimes identify them. Even now, as our motley individuals pose, we can see another figure in the Shadows. He is a military man in tattered uniform, and he sits on one of the boxes and crates that are on the stage and serve as furniture. He is the Honourable THE GENERAL. Note that besides the boxes and crates the stage is devoid of any props and sets.

After a few moments, when the audience has had the opportunity to savour the 'masterpiece', THE GENERAL comes to life and walks downstage in a dignified soldierly manner. He addresses the audience directly. But still the main focus remains on the 'masterpiece', particularly on THE PRESIDENT. THE GENERAL is given only secondary emphasis.

GENERAL [*indicating the masterpiece*]: There is art even in the humblest of things ... Yes, even in the most unassuming of situations. [*Pause.*] When I joined them, honouring a longstanding invitation to contribute my talents for the betterment of society, he was painting their picture ... A great artist rescued from the depth of despair though the Honourable the Minister of Culture's patriotic efforts. First there was a decree that art is only valid ... all art is valid only if it serves the interest of the people. And in what better way can the interests of the people be served, if not by creating masterpieces of their venerable leaders? The affairs of the state stood still while he immmortalised them on canvas. If this came out well, he was assured of continued employment, for he would be required to create a new painting every month. Earlier on, another decree had been passed ... No children would be born during this period. The old and the sick, lingering at the door of death, would suspend their transition into the world of ghosts. Fields would not be harvested, and rivers would not flow. All life would be in suspended animations until the painting was completed. And I, the General, the Honourable the General as I am officially called since joining this Honourable Cabinet, commander of our armed forces, second in command only to the Wise One, His Excellency the Father of the Nation, had to see to its implementation. That was my very first assignment. Later I was to become very adept at implementing decrees of this nature. You remember when the daughter of the Honourable the Minister of Agriculture was getting married? Yes, the Wedding of the Year ... or was it of the Decade now? The Wise One, Father of the Nation, instructed the Honourable the Minister of Information to decree that for the whole of that week nothing newsworthy in the country, and indeed in the world, would happen. Those who were going to commit murders and rapes waited in eagerness for the week to end. All international struggles, and all natural disasters, were on hold. All the news on radio, on television, and in the newspapers, was about the wedding. The wedding and only the wedding was to be reported ... and in meticulous detail too.

He marches to one of the boxes, and raps on it, using his fist as a gavel to call everyone to attention. Our 'masterpiece' is startled into life.

GENERAL [*with the flourish of a ringmaster announcing a circus act*]: Ladies and gentlemen of the Cabinet! Boys and girls! This meeting is called to order. Make way ... make way ... Here's the Supreme Commander, the One and Only, His Excellency the Wise One, Father of the Nation, Mr ... President!

They all look at THE PRESIDENT, *and give him the broadest smiles possible, which are nevertheless quite mechanical. As if responding to an unseen 'applause' sign they clap hands, also quite mechanically. He steps forward in a most gracious manner, smiling a most charming smile.*

PRESIDENT: Thank you ... thank you, ladies and gentlemen. The Honourable the General has called the meeting to order. We shall proceed with the business of the day.

HEALTH: Do we form a quorum?

AGRICULTURE: You always ask that.

HEALTH: I am a stickler for procedure, that's why.

PRESIDENT: Okay, okay, identify yourselves by naming your portfolios.

GENERAL: The Right Honourable the General, sir

AGRICULTURE: The Honourable the Minister of Agriculture, sir.

JUSTICE: The Honourable the Minister of Justice, sir.

HEALTH: The Honourable the Minister of Health, sir.

PRESIDENT: Is that all?

HEALTH: Obviously we don't form a quorum. A lot of the other honourable ministers are absent.

AGRICULTURE: Has that ever stopped us?

HEALTH: It's high time we followed proper procedure.

AGRICULTURE: Procedure, eh? Only because you know that the Father of the Nation will be discussing my daughter's wedding, you don't want the meeting to go on, eh?

JUSTICE: No need to quarrel about this. You know that when the Wise One is there it is a quorum, even if he is just alone.

PRESIDENT [*smiling benevolently*]: Now that we have cleared up that little matter we shall proceed with this special meeting. As you all know, our colleague's daughter is getting married in a week's time, and I take this opportunity to invite you all to the wedding. I have already sent the necessary instructions to the Ministry of Information and Broadcasting about the content of their programmes for the period of one week.

HEALTH: But sir, Your Excellency, if all the news in all the media for a whole week is about nothing but the wedding there surely won't be enough news to fill in all the time slots. The radio, for instance, broadcasts for twenty-four hours a day, and ...

JUSTICE [*to* AGRICULTURE]: She's bent on destroying you, my friend.

AGRICULTURE: She's such a nasty son of a bitch.

PRESIDENT: I do not want to see any of you being devoured by envy or jealousy. You have all served this government well. You have served your people well, in fact. From the days of our glorious revolution until our victory when we marched into the capital and took over the government. You did not falter. You were faithful and loyal. Right up to this day. It is not a special favour I am doing for my friend, the Honourable the Minister of Agriculture. It is a reward for his long, faithful and loyal service. I would do it for anyone of you if you had daughters who were getting married.

HEALTH: I am sorry if I sounded envious or jealous, Your Excellency. I was only wondering where the news will come from to fill all the time. I admit that my question is really due to my ignorance of the field of broadcasting. Perhaps if the Minister of Information and Broadcasting were here he'd be able to help me.

JUSTICE: Where does she get the gall to talk back to the Wise One like that?

AGRICULTURE [*with grudging admiration*]: She's one stubborn son of a bitch that one.

PRESIDENT: We have well qualified people who can create news. That's not our problem. They can work things out. They can have news on the groom, his life history, his achievements, interview his teachers from grade school right up to college ...

45

and the same can be done for the bride. Right there you have news to last you at least for three days. Then you profile the designer who has been imported to design the bridal gown.

AGRICULTURE: The Wise One is so wise.

PRESIDENT: And I am told he is a famous designer who has designed for film stars and first ladies of the world. That little fact must be highlighted in all news bulletins. Then in all the music programmes only wedding songs shall be played. You see, you can never run short of wedding material.

AGRICULTURE: Thank you, Wise One. May you see many more years, until you stoop and walk with a stick, Father of the Nation. My family shall forever be grateful.

PRESIDENT: And you, General, shall see to the implementation of this decree. See to it that every citizen throughout the land is in a jolly wedding mood. In shebeens and taverns let the discussions centre on the Wedding of the Decade. In discothèques and nightclubs let them dance to wedding marches.

HEALTH: Of the Decade, sir? What if one of the Cabinet members has a daughter who is getting married within the next ten years? You can't give the Minister of Agriculture the whole of this decade. Perhaps the Wedding of the Year, yes ... But of the Decade!

JUSTICE [to AGRICULTURE]: I told you.

AGRICULTURE: What a bitchy son of a bitch!

PRESIDENT [ignoring her]: And General, see to it that the Ministry of Works paves the road to our colleague's house ... make sure it's properly tarred. The road to the groom's house too.

GENERAL: I don't know if the Works people will take instructions from me since I am not their Minister.

PRESIDENT: You have the army behind you, General. Don't be timid to use it. Anyway, has no one of you heard from the Honourable the Minister of Works yet?

JUSTICE: No one, sir ... since they took him away.

AGRICULTURE: They took him, and never brought him back.

HEALTH: What a guy!

PRESIDENT: Indeed we have lost a great man there.

HEALTH: I have hope. They will bring him back one day.

JUSTICE: Maybe they have killed him.

HEALTH: You'd have such thoughts, wouldn't you? Maybe it's a wish, is it not?

AGRICULTURE: Cool down, darling. You know that when they take you in the morning, they bring you back in the evening. They never keep you for days on end.

HEALTH: Don't you darling me. He can't be dead! You just wish him dead! But he is alive. Do you hear me? He is alive!

JUSTICE: Why would we wish him dead? We all admired him. We all owe our wealth to his resourcefulness.

AGRICULTURE: He was a very clever one, wasn't he?

HEALTH: What a guy!

JUSTICE: What a guy? You never gave him the time of the day when he was here.

PRESIDENT: Yes, he was very resourceful. Always been like that. Even during the revolution. And when we took over the government I just had to make him Minister of Works.

AGRICULTURE: The best. The very best. Remember when the Pope visited our country?

The Ministers of AGRICULTURE *and* JUSTICE *laugh at the memory.* THE PRESIDENT *looks at them as if wondering what is so funny.* THE MINISTER OF HEALTH *pretends to be unconcerned, and* THE GENERAL *giggles uncomfortably but suddenly stops when* THE PRESIDENT *looks at him enquiringly.*

JUSTICE: Who can forget that, my friend? Who can forget that?

PRESIDENT: A private joke about the Holy Father, eh?

AGRICULTURE: Not about the Pope, sir. About the road.

JUSTICE: The dirt road that leads to the racecourse where the Pope addressed the multitudes.

PRESIDENT: Dirt road? There is no dirt road there. I was in the Popemobile with the Pope on that road. It's a tarred road.

AGRICULTURE: Exactly what we mean about the cleverness of the Honourable the Minister of Works, sir. When you announced that the pontiff was paying us a holy visit, there was not time nor money to tar the road that leads to the racecourse. And the racecourse was the only open field that was big enough to accommodate the multitudes who were expected to come and see the Holy Father.

PRESIDENT: And so? How did it get tarred?

JUSTICE: It was never tarred, sir. It was just painted black.

AGRICULTURE [*beside himself with laughter*]: And named after the Pope.

HEALTH: And when the rains came, they swept the black paint away. And opened up the gullies. There is no road, sir, and no one ever told you about this. And the Pope, poor fellow, I'm sure he is sitting over there in the Vatican boasting to his friends, 'Guess what, guys, I have a road in that country. My own road, named after me.' He does not know.

JUSTICE: Now don't you try to wash yourself clean. You were part of the Cabinet decision to paint the road.

PRESIDENT: And why was I not informed of this?

JUSTICE: We know that the mind of the Wise One is always occupied with heavy matters of state. We didn't want to bother you with petty things about roads when we had a genius like the Minister of Works to handle them.

HEALTH: What a guy!

AGRICULTURE: I find that so irritating I want to puke.

JUSTICE: Don't tell me you are jealous of a man who's not even here, my friend

AGRICULTURE: She's just trying to play hard to get. They always do that in the beginning. Trying to make me jealous by swooning over the Minister of Works who is now dead. But I'll get her, I promise you.

HEALTH: He's not dead! And you are not man enough to get me. You don't have what it takes. I am sure I'd sleep through it all.

PRESIDENT: And you, General, do you know anything about this?

GENERAL: No, sir. But I also doubt if he's dead, unless of course you think he's dead, sir.

PRESIDENT: About the road, man. Did you know about it?

GENERAL: I did attend the meeting, yes, sir.

PRESIDENT: And you did not even confide in me? Well, at least the road did impress the pontiff, and so did the beautiful houses.

JUSTICE: There are no houses, sir.

PRESIDENT: Of course there are houses. On both sides of the road. Lovely double-storeyed houses in sunny colours.

AGRICULTURE: Again the brilliant work of the Honourable the Minister of Works.

JUSTICE: What you and the Holy Father saw were just the fronts of houses. The same kind of things they use when they shoot movies.

AGRICULTURE: Film sets made of masonite boards.

PRESIDENT [taken aback]: And the people at the windows? Surely there were people waving at me and the Pope.

JUSTICE: Some windows, yes, there were people waving. They were really standing on a pile of garbage behind the masonite boards. Children waving little flags. Sweet old ladies waving rosaries.

AGRICULTURE: But most of them were painted faces … happy faces with broad smiles … We didn't have enough children and old ladies to stand at all the windows. It was too hot and many people were not keen to sacrifice. Those who did, we had to offer something in return.

JUSTICE: Whatever happed to 'ask not what your country will do for you …'

PRESIDENT [laughing]: I am devastated!

JUSTICE: We didn't want to bother you with mundane things, sir.

PRESIDENT: And all the time I thought it was a new housing project. There were flats and apartments and stores. I was wondering how I was left out when a percentage was negotiated with the contractors, and why I didn't see my bank account unexpectedly bulging. I should have known better. He would never even dream of leaving the man who created him out of any bribes-for-contracts deal. He was indeed brilliant, wasn't he?

HEALTH: What a guy!

PRESIDENT: Maybe when the Minister of Culture is brought back he'll have news of him.

AGRICULTURE: That snivelling son of a bitch. He's the one they should keep instead of the Minister of Works

HEALTH: You hate him, don't you? Because he's refined and cultured and sensitive and loving.

AGRICULTURE: He's a whining bastard, that's what he is. He is not a man. Why you like to pay so much attention to him I'll never understand.

JUSTICE: Maybe just to make you jealous, my friend.

AGRICULTURE: You are right. She wants me just as much as I want her.

HEALTH: You are a joke of a man. I doubt if you even have it.

AGRICULTURE [*desperately*]: I want you! Is that too much to ask?

HEALTH: You want every little skirt that passes by.

JUSTICE: Is that not what women were made for … to be wanted?

We hear the sound of chains, of keys, and of a heavy metal door opening. Suddenly our motley individuals are alert, and are dead scared. The unseen door opens, and a beam of light rushes into the cell. Then a grotesque and menacing shadow maps itself on the beam. The honourable members cringe back. A haggard MINISTER OF CULTURE is thrown into the cell. He is even more tattered than the members we have already met. The heavy metal door closes again. The keys, and the chains, sound. Everyone rushes to the MINISTER OF CULTURE. He seems to be dazed for a moment. The PRESIDENT looks at him sadly, then retires to the Shadows. The GENERAL dutifully follows him.

HEALTH: Poor fellow! What did they do to you?

AGRICULTURE: Whoa! They gave him the works. They really did.

JUSTICE: Ask him if he heard anything of the Minister of Works.

HEALTH: Is that all you can think about? Can't you see what they have done to him?

JUSTICE [*contemptuously indicating* CULTURE]: He's alive, isn't he? They took the Minister of Works and never returned him. Shouldn't I be concerned?

The MINISTER OF CULTURE stands up and looks around in confusion. He is terribly bruised, and seems to be lost.

HEALTH: Don't worry, you are back among friends.

CULTURE *bursts out laughing.*

CULTURE: Today is the day they are not giving us any food.

HEALTH: Poor fellow, he's delirious.

CULTURE: Seriously. I heard them say so. And you know that I love you. But I cannot afford to love anyone now. Not after they handled me the way they did. I am not capable of loving, even you, beautiful princess.

HEALTH: Don't worry. You will recover.

AGRICULTURE: And soon he'll be fawning over you like the puppy he is.

JUSTICE: All I am worried about is whether he betrayed the cause or not. Anything is possible with him. He's a weakling.

AGRICULTURE: Did you betray the cause?

CULTURE: Of course not! What do you take me for, man?

HEALTH: He wouldn't be here if he'd betrayed the cause. They would have taken him and bathed him in myrrh and showered him with gifts of precious stones. That's what they do to those who betray the cause. In any case, whatever you think of him he's always been our staunchest member, in spite of suffering numerous insults from the likes of you.

CULTURE: But for sure there is a traitor among us.

AGRICULTURE: Are you sure?

JUSTICE: How do you know?

CULTURE: During the interrogation they came up with things that should be known only to us. They know everything, man. All they wanted me to do was to confirm whether it was true or not.

JUSTICE: And did you confirm?

CULTURE: I denied, man. I denied everything. In spite of the torture I did not betray the cause.

HEALTH: You see, I told you.

CULTURE: They could not break me. They will never break me. [*Speaking into their faces.*] Do you hear that, you righteous guardian of our stomachs, and you my learned friend? I was there with them, but they could not break me.

JUSTICE: What was today's speciality?

CULTURE: A combination of things. [*Laughing*.] First they made me a ball in a game of football or rugby. They threw me around, and kicked me, and scored with me quite a few times. Mind you, you are naked all the time when they do that.

AGRICULTURE: Is that something new, this football game?

JUSTICE: They are known to do that sometimes.

CULTURE: Then they kept me standing for hours on end until my eyes began to pop out. I stood naked for the whole day. At intervals they came to spit at me. Everybody, even their children, showered me with saliva and phlegm. Then they sat all around me and hurled insults and all sorts of verbal abuse. When that failed to break me they threw faeces at me.

JUSTICE: So now it's faeces, eh? It used to be mud.

AGRICULTURE: How do you know? They haven't called you yet.

JUSTICE: I have studied their methods. That's what a good Minister of Justice does ... make an in depth study of torture methods. Never know when they may come in handy.

CULTURE: It started with mud, I learn. But now it's definitely faeces. [*He suddenly breaks down.*] Then they attacked my genitals with a pair of pliers. When I was bleeding they got their dogs to lap blood from my body.

His bravado is now gone, and he weeps uncontrollably. The two men look at him with disgust and contempt. The woman takes him to some corner and smothers him with hugs.

HEALTH: Everything will be all right. This nightmare will be over. We'll all go home and be happy again.

CULTURE [*crying*]: I'll never love again, beautiful princess. They humiliated me so much ... they forced a rod up my anus as I was given electric shocks ... they kicked and punched me ... they pushed needles under my nails ...

HEALTH [*rocking him like a baby*]: It is a terrible life to be a minister. A life of sacrifice and humiliation. A life of pain and sadness. An adage of our people says that a chief is a receptacle of all faeces. So is a minister, I add. It is our lot, we the servants of the people. To be spat at and humiliated and pilloried at the Market Square. But you will get over it. We'll all get over it. We'll surely love again. Even if we never do ... remember ... the Wise One ... he is a very benevolent man. His heart is overflowing with love. He has the capacity to love for us all. We can sit back and let him love on our behalf.

Lights fade to dark as she rocks the sobbing MINISTER OF CULTURE *to sleep.*

Scene Two

The spot is on the MINISTER OF CULTURE. *He is sitting on one of the boxes and is pulling out the petals of an imaginary flower. The rest of the members are sleeping in grotesque positions in the Shadows. The* MINISTER OF AGRICULTURE *wakes up, and creeps up on the* MINISTER OF CULTURE.

CULTURE: She loves me, she loves me not ... she loves me, she loves me not ... she loves me, she loves me not ...

AGRICULTURE: What are you doing?

CULTURE [*startled and hiding the flower*]: Oh, nothing.

AGRICULTURE: It's about her, isn't it?

CULTURE [*mortified*]: None of your business.

AGRICULTURE [*laughing*]: How stupid can you get! How dumb! And what stupid nonsense ... 'she loves me, she loves me not ...' What rubbish!

CULTURE: We all know that she does not want you, however much you spew your venom on me.

AGRICULTURE: And you think she wants you? You are just her little puppy as far as she is concerned. Woof! Woof! Sniff! Sniff!

At this moment the MINISTER OF HEALTH, *who has just woken up, joins them.*

HEALTH: Boys, boys, boys, what is the problem now?

The MINISTER OF CULTURE *climbs down from the box, and kneels in front of the* MINISTER OF HEALTH.

CULTURE: May I wash your feet, beautiful princess?

HEALTH [*amused*]: With what? We don't have any water here.

CULTURE: With my tongue. [*To* AGRICULTURE.] See if you can top that.

AGRICULTURE: Me, I don't lick your feet. I give you the time of your life as only a man can do.

He pinches her bottom.

HEALTH: You do that again, I am going to cut your thing ... which is already not there in any case.

AGRICULTURE [*scandalised*]: You like to impugn my manhood, don't you? You think you can castrate me with your words?

HEALTH: My tongue cannot do what nature has already done so effectively.

CULTURE [*standing up*]: I have this recurring dream, beautiful princess ... I walk in a garden full of flowers ... hand in hand with you.

AGRICULTURE: So corny.

HEALTH: Shows how crude you are. To you, of course, flower gardens would be corny. Tell me more about your garden, little prince.

AGRICULTURE [*laughs*]: Bah! Little prince! That's a new one, that. Just like a puppy's name.

HEALTH: Well, if he calls me beautiful princess I might as well call him little prince. Or even handsome prince. How do you like that?

CULTURE [*quite flattered*]: Well, it's just a flower garden. And blossoms scent the air. Many varieties of flowers. From large yellow sunflowers that smile at the moon, to small Easter flowers that fill the ground with deep yellowness.

HEALTH: It is a yellow garden then?

CULTURE: Yellow roses, yellow dahlias, yellow zinnias, yellow petunias.

AGRICULTURE: Ha! There are no yellow petunias. They only come in white, pink, purple or red.

CULTURE: Well, in my garden there are yellow petunias. And there are yellow bees that are so large that a child can ride on their backs.

HEALTH [*sweetly*]: It is a beautiful garden.

CULTURE: You make it more beautiful when you walk with me in it, beautiful princess, especially when you are wearing a yellow dress, and I'm in my yellow suit.

AGRICULTURE: Let's see what the Father of the Nation will say about this.

He goes to the Shadows.

CULTURE: In my garden pigs are grazing peacefully.

HEALTH: They are yellow too?

CULTURE: They are white. Pigs can be white, it really doesn't make that much difference. Tell you what, your yellow dress can have white polks dots too. We can always mingle the yellow with a little white whenever we feel like it.

The MINISTER OF AGRICULTURE *comes back with the* PRESIDENT, *the* GENERAL *and the* MINISTER OF JUSTICE. *The* GENERAL *leads the way, marching like a sergeant-at-arms, and announces the arrival of the* PRESIDENT.

GENERAL: Mr … President!

PRESIDENT: What's this I hear that you are now poaching on the Honourable the Minister of Agriculture's turf?

HEALTH: Who does he say poached on his turf?

JUSTICE: Do you forget that it is crass to ask the Wise One questions? He asks the questions, you give the answers.

AGRICULTURE: They did, Father of the Nation. They were discussing gardens which is my portfolio as Minister of Agriculture.

PRESIDENT: I am sure you understand that for the smooth running of the country we cannot afford to interfere in each others' portfolios. Otherwise we would have anarchy in this Cabinet and indeed, in the country. All horticultural matters are in the jurisdiction of the Honourable the Minister of Agriculture.

CULTURE: It's just a private flower garden, Father of the Nation.

PRESIDENT: Flower garden? That's even worse than I thought. Now listen very carefully all of you. I hereby make this decree without fear or favour: All flower gardens are banned. Henceforth no one will plant flowers. People don't eat flowers. In our fields let us see only the luxuriant leaves of wheat, tobacco and hops. We need to be self-sufficient in things that keep body and soul together, and that can be exported in exchange for the little luxuries that are essential to sustain the lives of those who sacrifice to lead this country on the path of freedom and prosperity.

JUSTICE: The Wise One has spoken.

AGRICULTURE: Let it be so.

CULTURE [*mechanically*]: The Wise One is so wise.

HEALTH: Wise One, Father of the Nation, I salute your benevolence. And your wisdom. I bow my head, Wise One, and ask to be allowed to bring to the attention of the Honourable Members the fact that flowers are cultural. If the Honourable Minister of Culture is deprived of the right to enjoy his flower garden, he is deprived of the right to function in his capacity as Minister of Culture.

AGRICULTURE: Can't he speak for himself?

PRESIDENT: Whose culture, if I may ask? Surely not ours? Flowers are against our culture.

JUSTICE: In any case we agreed at a very special meeting that culture is not on the agenda. We have more important things to talk about. We want to talk about contracts ... contracts for housing our civil servants, contracts for road construction to centres of government and to the residences of the national leaders, contracts for the supply of private jets, contracts for constructing international airports and conference centres, contracts for the construction of new courthouses, jails and offices for my ministry, contracts for the construction of new mansions for us esteemed rulers. Contracts! We want to talk about development and national reconstruction.

AGRICULTURE: Hear! Hear! Although you forgot my ministry in your long list of development projects.

JUSTICE: If my memory serves me well, the Wise One decreed that in fact the Honourable the Minister of Culture should play an active role in killing culture by destroying all the people who have dances, and who have carvings.

PRESIDENT: I don't remember that decree, although it doesn't sound like a bad idea.

CULTURE: There was never such a decree, Father of the Nation.

HEALTH: It is of his own composition, Wise One. You can ask Right Honourable General, who is the implementer of all your decrees.

PRESIDENT: General?

GENERAL: No such decree, sir. There was a Cabinet decision that culture is not on the national agenda. But there was never a decree to kill producers of cultural products.

JUSTICE: My mistake. I could have sworn there was such a decree.

HEALTH: Why do we have a Minister of Culture at all if culture is not on the agenda?

PRESIDENT: Because it is fashionable to have a Minister of Culture. And that closes that subject. The decree on the flower garden has been made and cannot be unmade. Pardon me, Honourable Members, it is time for my introspection.

He climbs on one of the boxes and sits there, occupied with his stately thoughts. THE GENERAL *follows him, and sits next to him.*

AGRICULTURE: But I must admit, the Minister of Culture can serve a very useful purpose.

JUSTICE: You don't say?

AGRICULTURE: He is a man of culture. He can dance for us.

JUSTICE: Yes. He can dance to relieve the boredom of our long Cabinet meetings.

AGRICULTURE: C'mon Culture ... dance!

HEALTH: You can't be serious!

JUSTICE: He is going to dance.

CULTURE: I am not dancing for you, or for anyone.

THE MINISTER OF JUSTICE *prods his bottom with his finger.*

JUSTICE: Dance, Culture, dance!

CULTURE: See what they are doing, Your Excellency!

HEALTH: Can't you stop them, Wise One?

PRESIDENT: No, they are just playing.

HEALTH: No, they are not playing! They like to bully him.

PRESIDENT [*angry at being disturbed*]: Just dance and get it over with.

JUSTICE: The Wise One has spoken, Culture-boy. Dance your heart out.

CULTURE: If the Wise One says so.

HEALTH: This is an unnecessary humiliation of a man who has served the President so faithfully.

The Ministers of AGRICULTURE *and* JUSTICE *clap hands and shout, while the* MINISTER OF CULTURE *reluctantly dances. The* MINISTER OF HEALTH *looks away in disgust. The* PRESIDENT *is busy with his brooding, while the* GENERAL *looks on disinterestedly.*

JUSTICE & AGRICULTURE [*clapping hands*]: Go, go, go Culture! Go, go, go Culture!

The sound of the key, the chains and the metal door. The dance suddenly stops and everyone is scared. The flood of light and menacing shadow.

AGRICULTURE [*to* JUSTICE]: He is calling you.

JUSTICE: No! No! He pointed at you. [*To* CULTURE] He is calling you!

CULTURE: Oh, no … not me again. He called me yesterday. It is someone else's turn now!

HEALTH: Oh, my God! It's me. He is calling me. How can it be?

JUSTICE: How can it not be? Do you want to be treated as special just because you are a woman? And they say they want equality!

CULTURE: No! Take me instead! Take me instead of her! Let me go through it again instead of the beautiful princess!

HEALTH *screams, and drags herself up.*

HEALTH: Have mercy! Please have mercy on me!

The menacing shadow disappears with the MINISTER OF HEALTH, *and the metal door closes. The sound of the keys and chains. The remaining members are numb for a moment.*

JUSTICE: Whew! That was a close one.

CULTURE: Maybe they won't be as harsh on her. She is a lady. They've got to treat her like a lady.

AGRICULTURE: She has said to me many times that she is not a lady, she is a woman.

CULTURE: Because you use the word 'lady' patronisingly

JUSTICE: Never patronise a woman, my friend. Condescend, yes. It is a fact that we are superior to them. We can only treat them with condescension.

AGRICULTURE: Anyway, that's going to teach her a thing or two. She will know that being a minister is not all fun and games. I bet when she comes back she'll know how to eat humble pie.

JUSTICE: Yeah. If she wants to play a man's game she must take her medicine like a man. I now doubt if we did the right thing by promoting her into the Cabinet.

PRESIDENT: The disadvantages of having her here are far outweighed by the benefits we'll reap from her presence.

AGRICULTURE: They are slow in coming, these benefits, Wise One. The Daughters of the Revolution continue to be a nuisance.

CULTURE: So is that why she was made a minister, to control the Daughters of the Revolution?

PRESIDENT: We made her a minister as an indication that we are an enlightened government. The fact that that would silence the Daughters of the Revolution by showing them that we had a woman in the Cabinet was supposed only to be the icing on our cake. A by-product of our enlightenment.

JUSTICE: Our plan didn't work then. The Daughters of the Revolution are still at it. She should have reverted to her womanly role after the revolution.

PRESIDENT: They are at it again?

AGRICULTURE: Demonstrating and polluting this whole city with the stench of filthy ideas.

JUSTICE: Like the stench of the buckets of faeces in this cell.

AGRICULTURE: At least we live with it here, and we are so used to it that if it were not here we would all get sick.

JUSTICE: You are right, my friend. I have noticed that since they let us take the buckets out once a month to the sewerage dump, on those days when they are empty we become quite uncomfortable and fidgety. Some of us even throw up.

PRESIDENT: Forget faeces! What do they want now, the Daughters of the Revolution?

JUSTICE: They say first we took their Bibles and their guns. Now we want to take their slogans too.

PRESIDENT: They never gave us a chance. We were attacked the day we took over the government. On the very first day they were already making demands ... they were already talking of the failure of the revolution ... they were already shouting to the world in their shrill voices that the revolution had been hijacked. 'Give us a change to fail before you start attacking us,' we pleaded. When they didn't listen we just had to be ruthless. They can't blame us now that we want to deprive them of their slogans.

JUSTICE: We should have been ruthless right from the beginning. Justice can only be served though ruthlessness. We inherited this revolution from those who did the actual fighting. We now own it. They refuse to accept that at their peril.

AGRICULTURE [*laughing*]: They have now taken to marching naked in the Market Square, singing songs of praise about the Wise One, Father of the Nation.

PRESIDENT: Songs, eh? That's the jurisdiction of the Minister of Culture. What did you do about it?

CULTURE: I did not know what to do. They have become very fierce. When they march men run away.

JUSTICE: They are women still. They need to be disciplined. They need to know who wears the pants in this country.

CULTURE: I even asked the Right the Honourable the General for his assistance.

PRESIDENT: General?

GENERAL: I could not do much to quell their rowdy behaviour, sir. Since we adopted the National Policy of Benevolence it has become increasingly difficult for me to use force in full view of the populace.

PRESIDENT: People who are keen to disrupt good governance, law and order do not deserve our benevolence. [*To* CULTURE.] And you, you just listen for subversion in their songs. It is your work as Minister of Culture. Read between the lines in all their activities. If they shout, 'Long live Your Excellency!' there might be 'Death to the President!' somewhere between the lines. And why do they sing my praises only when they are naked? Bludgeon them into silence. That's what a good Minister of Culture does.

JUSTICE: Yes. Those who disagree with us we bludgeon into submission. It always works.

CULTURE: They will not be silenced. They are ready to die for their beliefs. They say that a truth that is worth living for is worth dying for.

PRESIDENT: Truth? What do they know of truth? Where has it ever existed as a constant? Yesterday were they not heroes when they stood their ground in the revolution? Today are they not villains when they insist they want a piece of the national dream?

CULTURE: The Wise One is so wise. We were taught that truth is forever. It never changes at anyone's convenience. What was true centuries ago is true today.

AGRICULTURE: Truth and the Daughters of the Revolution are strangers.

PRESIDENT: You know, of course, that it is not true that truth is forever. Not many centuries ago the church burnt those who disagreed with its doctrines at the stake. It was the truth of the time that they were witches, and it was the truth of the time that witches had to be set alight and die in flames.

JUSTICE: If God's word is ephemeral …

CULTURE: God's word?

JUSTICE: The church is the eyes, the ears and the mouth of God on earth. It is the interpreter of God's word. If the church of God can have ephemeral truth, who are we to have eternal truth?

CULTURE: That means to die for today's truth may be to die for tomorrow's lie!

This discovery greatly disturbs them.

AGRICULTURE: Dying for nothing!

JUSTICE: Dying for rubbish! When people ask you the next day, what will you say you died for?

CULTURE: Then why are we here if our truth is only for today? Why do we go through all the pain and humiliation?

PRESIDENT: What is important is that at the moment, as we speak, ours is the truth that must prevail. It should not bother us what tomorrow will think of it. Even I, Wise One, cannot make truth to be eternal. The Honourable the Minister of Justice has observed, with wisdom typical only of me, that even God's own truth is ephemeral.

JUSTICE: I apologise, Father of the Nation. I should have let you utter that wise observation, which was in fact based on your wisdom.

CULTURE: What does all this mean as far as the Daughters of the Revolution are concerned?

PRESIDENT: It means theirs was the truth yesterday when they stood in the line of fire and fought in the revolution. Today we, the inheritors of that revolution, must be resolved to crush them to smithereens. The Daughters of the Revolution are yesterday's news. We are today's.

CULTURE: My worry, Wise One, is that if we crush them through force of arms overseas newspapers will write about it and that will be a blight on our National Policy of Benevolence. We have put a lot of work into this policy. We are beginning to win over the populace. People are singing about the bountiful benevolence of the leader, the Supreme Commander, the One and Only ...

JUSTICE: Except that of course those who sing are on the state payroll. So don't take credit and pretend to the Wise One that they sing because you have effectively done your work as Minister of Culture. However I do agree that we must find a way to crush these mad women without attracting the unnecessary attention of the world community. Our police have a reputation for brutality already ...

PRESIDENT: I have been meaning to talk to the General about this.

The police need to do their work as they have done before. They need to suppress uprisings unhindered. But we cannot afford to have the populace thinking that the police are brutal. It goes against the whole idea of benevolence. I want yo u, General, and you, Minister of Justice, to take immediate action. Buy them new uniforms that are brighter and invoke friendliness. Change their dull militaristic drill to a much more rhythmic one ... a much more dancey one ... Let the populace see that it's not only the Daughters of the Revolution who know how to dance.

AGRICULTURE: I do not intend to question our great National Policy of Benevolence which, after all, was founded through the wisdom of the Father of the Nation. But I strongly feel that we need a catastrophe to bring our existence to the attention of the world. As long as we are benevolent, as long as there is peace, they will not hear of us. They will not know of us.

CULTURE: Since even the Wise One cannot call upon a natural disaster ... an earthquake that kills hundreds, or a flood ... maybe we ourselves should do something ... should create a catastrophe.

JUSTICE: I have an idea ...

CULTURE: You cannot have an idea. Only His Excellency the Father of the Nation can have an idea. You can utter some words about something. They only become an idea when the Wise One thinks they are good enough to adopt and shape into an idea – his idea. That's the first lesson I learnt when I joined this Cabinet.

He laughs proudly at having at last struck a blow against the MINISTER OF JUSTICE, *who glares at him with hate.*

AGRICULTURE [*to* JUSTICE]: The son of a bitch has successfully disgraced you in front of His Excellency, my friend.

JUSTICE: My thoughts are that next time the Daughters of the Revolution march at the Market Square we should mow them down with machine guns. That will be a catastrophe that will call the attention of the world to us. They will know of our existence.

AGRICULTURE: Very clever, my friend. Killing two birds with

one stone, so to speak. Getting rid of the Daughters of the Revolution, and putting us on the world map.

CULTURE [*to* JUSTICE]: Your own aged mother is one of the Daughters of the Revolution!

JUSTICE: She is a traitor, and she's none of your business!

CULTURE: What are we saying? First we say we cannot use force on them because of world opinion. Now we say we are going to use force on them for world opinion.

JUSTICE: Too complicated for your feeble mind. Better you confine yourself to song and dance.

AGRICULTURE: Well, my friend, sometimes these things need elaboration, so that when these decisions are implemented there should be no mistake. I am really asking on behalf of those who will have to implement our decisions.

CULTURE: Well?

The Ministers of CULTURE *and* AGRICULTURE *look at the* MINISTER OF JUSTICE *for the answer, but none is forthcoming. He can only display his confusion.*

PRESIDENT [*smiling benevolently at each of them*]: We are the creators of our own little truths, remember? We'll hold a television interview ... we'll call the international press ... we'll condemn the killings, and make it clear that they contravened our National Policy of Benevolence. We'll tell them that they were by and large self-inflicted by the Daughters of the Revolution themselves, who had disguised themselves as our national army, with the view of calling attention to themselves, and of besmirching the name of this benevolent government.

GENERAL: It shall be so.

JUSTICE, AGRICULTURE, CULTURE: The Wise One is so wise!

The sound of the keys and the chains. The Honourable Members are scared, and huddle together in trepidation. Only the PRESIDENT *stands his ground bravely.*

PRESIDENT: Are they bringing her back so soon?

JUSTICE: Maybe she is the traitor. She is the betrayer of the cause.

CULTURE: I refuse to believe that. She can't be the traitor. She is steadfast in her commitment to the cause. I can vouch for her any day.

JUSTICE: And why would we take your word? You might be in it together. After all you are lovers and you walk together in flower gardens.

AGRICULTURE: They are not lovers. He is her puppy.

JUSTICE: She must be the traitor.

AGRICULTURE: If she is I'll personally break her bones, one by one.

JUSTICE: It's gone! The terrible sound of the chains and keys is gone.

They all laugh in relief.

CULTURE: Maybe it was just our imagination.

JUSTICE: Imagination, eh? Do you think we have time to have imagination, like the crazy cultural people you deal with, creators of meaningless lies from imagination? We deal with reality here, man! With brave facts!

CULTURE [*laughing at* JUSTICE]: You deal with facts, and you are a brave man, but you were scared like the rest of us.

JUSTICE: Who, me? Scared?

PRESIDENT: There is no shame in being scared.

AGRICULTURE: Only the Wise One has the right not to be scared.

PRESIDENT: Sometimes it's brave to be scared.

JUSTICE: Well, I must admit … I am scared. Every time the door opens I pee in my pants. Just a few burning drops. Then he calls someone else … relief floods my chest … a feeling of elation overwhelms me … I become happy and kind to everyone. [*To* CULTURE.] That's why I am being nice to you even though you have been on my case all day long.

CULTURE: They did terrible things to me, but I did not pee in my pants.

JUSTICE: You are not brave, of course. The Wise One has told us that fear is an expression of bravery.

The chains and keys again. The Honourable Members suddenly stop their banter, and are filled with fear. The door opens, and a YOUNG MAN *is thrown into the cell. He is well groomed and is quite colourful in the latest of casual fashion, or what is sometimes referred to as street fashion. They all look at him in amazement. The door closes again. Then the chains and the keys.*

JUSTICE: Who the hell is this?

PRESIDENT: Who are you, young man? And why are you here?

The YOUNG MAN *does not respond. He stands up, brushes the dust off his clothes with his hands, and walks to one of the boxes. He sits there moping, ignoring everyone.*

AGRICULTURE: Hey, boy, you answer when the Wise One speaks to you.

CULTURE: His face looks quite familiar.

JUSTICE: What is your business here, boy?

PRESIDENT: Perhaps he is deaf, or dumb.

AGRICULTURE: Do you know who the Wise One is, boy? Where do you get the cheek to ignore him?

JUSTICE: Maybe he has been sent to spy on us.

CULTURE: Maybe they are becoming desperate. They are unable to break us in spite of the fact that they have a traitor among us, and in spite of their torture and humiliation. But, really, he's just a young man. He doesn't look like a spy to me.

JUSTICE: Why should he be so young when we have grown so old in the service of this country without seeing the light of day? What right has he to be so young?

AGRICULTURE: He is young. He has come to overthrow us.

JUSTICE: Have you come to overthrow us, boy?

AGRICULTURE: Who sent you, boy?

JUSTICE: Maybe we should let the General give him the works.

They surround the YOUNG MAN *threateningly. But he does not seem to be bothered. He looks at them with contempt.*

JUSTICE: Boy, do you want us to get the General to work on you?

AGRICULTURE: Just let me give him one good one with my fist. It will sure open his mouth.

CULTURE: No, please! He has not done anything!

JUSTICE: How do you know he has not done anything? First you interfere in the Honourable the Minister of Agriculture's portfolio by creating gardens, now you want to interfere in my portfolio as Minister of Justice. When has anyone ever been innocent, unless and until my ministry declared him innocent?

AGRICULTURE: Yes, everyone is guilty until they are declared innocent through the guidance of the Wise One.

CULTURE: You are making that up, aren't you?

JUSTICE: You call yourself an Honourable Member of the Cabinet, yet you are ignorant of our rules and of our procedure. You do not know what the rule of law entails. You do not know about law and order. You do not even know the decrees that have been passed by the Wise One over the years.

AGRICULTURE: The boy is a danger to our existence, Wise One. Allow us to kill him.

The Ministers of AGRICULTURE *and* JUSTICE *charge at the* YOUNG MAN, *but they stop in their tracks when he faces them defiantly.*

PRESIDENT: Do not touch him. Remember, we do not know who he is. Until we know his mission we remain benevolent.

GENERAL: The Wise One has spoken.

ALL: He has spoken!

Lights fade to dark.

Scene Three

The dull yellowish light of the night. The YOUNG MAN *is sitting on one of the boxes, moping. The* PRESIDENT *is sitting on another box, brooding. His bandaged leg is outstretched, and the* GENERAL *tries to whisk flies away from it with his open hand. The other Ministers are just sitting around, bored.*

AGRICULTURE: Stubborn sons of a bitch, eh General?

GENERAL: Yes. They keep on coming back.

JUSTICE: What's with them anyway? They should be sleeping at this time.

AGRICULTURE: That's the problem with these summer flies. They just never do what they are supposed to do at the time they are supposed to do it.

CULTURE: But you must admit though, they are so beautiful to look at. See them hovering over the buckets of our human waste, or over the leg of the Wise One, and admire their glowing bodies in metallic green. Listen to their buzzz ... zzz ... like honey bees. Only theirs has the sharp whine of sorrow.

JUSTICE: Sorrow at creating all this misery for us.

CULTURE: Damnit! When will they bring her back?

AGRICULTURE: They should give the Father of the Nation a break, and hover only over the buckets.

CULTURE: She's been gone for the whole day. God knows what they are doing to her.

AGRICULTURE: Can't you shut up about her!

JUSTICE: I think it is time to change the bandages.

AGRICULTURE: Who's going to do it? The Minister of Health is not here.

CULTURE: So when you want her to work you worry about her not being here?

AGRICULTURE: It is her jurisdiction as Minister of Health to change His Excellency's bandages.

JUSTICE: More importantly she is a woman, and it is her work to take care of men. If God didn't want her to change bandages he would have made her a man.

CULTURE: Well, he's not here.

JUSTICE: Get the boy to do it.

AGRICULTURE: Hey, boy, come and change the bandages!

The YOUNG MAN *does not budge.*

AGRICULTURE: The son of a bitch is as stubborn as these flies.

JUSTICE: We'll have to force him to do it. Boy, I'll give you five seconds to drag your rear end here and change these bandages!

AGRICULTURE: We'll have to drag him here screaming. We'll

have to kick him into action. Who the hell does he think he is anyway? Coming here, and just sitting there as if he is the Wise One himself.

CULTURE: You can't use force on him. The Wise One said not to.

JUSTICE: Well, well, I think then you'll have to do it.

CULTURE: Use force? Never!

JUSTICE: No. Change the bandages.

CULTURE: Who? Me? No, no, sir, my portfolio is Culture not Health.

AGRICULTURE: Health ... Culture ... What's the difference? After all you claim to be closer to her than anyone of us here. So you must do her job.

CULTURE: You do it. Health is much closer to Agriculture than to Culture.

The PRESIDENT *glares at the* MINISTER OF CULTURE, *then breaks into a benevolent smile.*

CULTURE: Okay, I'll do it. It will be an honour to change His Excellency's bandages.

He unwraps the bandages.

CULTURE: The whole leg is riddled with sores.

JUSTICE: Don't let the flies sit on them, you dweeb!

AGRICULTURE: They are having such a good time, I am sure they are not looking forward to the healing of those sores.

CULTURE: The flies are not worried about that. These are not sores that can heal.

PRESIDENT: That is subversive talk. So that's why my sores don't heal, because you don't wish them to heal?

CULTURE: Not me, Your Excellency. The flies.

JUSTICE: Ha! Now he blames the flies.

The chains and the keys. The door opens. The menacing shadow. Obviously even though it is night the light on the other side is much brighter, for it rushes into the dull cell. The MINISTER OF HEALTH *is thrown into the cell. All is still for a while, with the Cabinet members expecting the shadow to go away and lock the door after it. But the shadow does not go. At the same time the* MINISTER OF HEALTH *stands up, and is fuming. She walks with a limp. The* MINISTER OF CULTURE *rushes to her.*

CULTURE: Oh, what have they done to you, beautiful princess?
HEALTH [*pushing him away*]: Get out of my way!
JUSTICE: He won't go.
AGRICULTURE: He's calling one of us.
JUSTICE: It can't be. They never call us at night. Torture is a thing of the day.
CULTURE: Maybe they have grown impatient with our resistance and have decided to torture and humiliate us twenty-four hours a day.
JUSTICE: He's calling you, my friend. He is pointing at you.
AGRICULTURE: He is pointing at you. He's calling you, not me.
JUSTICE: Maybe he is calling the boy. Boy, he's calling you!
AGRICULTURE: He's becoming impatient, my friend. The sooner you go, the better, otherwise they'll be more vicious to you.
JUSTICE: My God! He is calling me! Please have mercy on me!

He drags himself out, screaming. The shadow disappears with the light, and the heavy metal door is violently slammed. The chains and the keys. The MINISTER OF HEALTH *sees the* YOUNG MAN.

HEALTH: And who is this one? Who are you?

The YOUNG MAN *does not answer.*

AGRICULTURE: He's the boy who has been sent to spy on us.
HEALTH: Did he tell you that?
AGRICULTURE: Of course not. Spies wouldn't be so daft as to announce that they are spies.
HEALTH: Why would they send someone like him to spy on us when they already have a traitor among us? They know everything about us that there is to know. One of you is a bloody traitor!
CULTURE: That's what I have been saying too. Their interrogations are the interrogations of people who know something about us. We have been betrayed!
HEALTH: They even know our dreams.
AGRICULTURE: If he is not a spy, then who is he?

The MINISTER OF HEALTH *walks closer to the* YOUNG MAN, *and examines him from head to toe closely. She is obviously in pain, and moves her muscles with difficulty.*

CULTURE: Are you all right, beautiful princess?

HEALTH: What is it to you? Why don't you shut up and leave me alone?

CULTURE: She is not herself. She has never spoken to me like that. Oh, what I'll do to them if I get the chance. When this is over and we've triumphed they will pay for this.

AGRICULTURE: She is doing what she should have done to you a long time ago. You are a pest that she tolerates only for her amusement.

CULTURE: Tell him it is not so, beautiful princess. He is the pest with dirty thoughts all the time.

HEALTH: Won't you two shut your diseased mouths, your mouths that drip syphilis.

CULTURE [*hurt*]: Oh, beautiful princess!

AGRICULTURE: Dirty thoughts, eh? Just because I want what any normal man in my circumstances would want. Just because I am not a eunuch! She is a woman, isn't she? Ha! Look, she is limping. I can see it now. They must have done it to her. And to think that she won't give us a little bit. She won't even let me touch her. Yeah, they have done it to her. They've given it to her hard and fast.

HEALTH: You never give up, do you?

AGRICULTURE: It's been such a long time without the balm of lovemaking, I think I am regressing to virginity.

HEALTH: Take heart. You are saving some lucky woman the frustrations of unfulfilment.

AGRICULTURE: Don't insult my manhood, lady. I want to bathe my battered soul in the deep night of your body … your tortured and humiliated body …

PRESIDENT: Will my leg stay like this, unbandaged for every little fly to defecate on … while you babble off your greed for each others' bodies? Was the Honourable Minister of Culture not supposed to be attending to my sores?

CULTURE: I am sorry, Wise One. We were distracted by the arrival of the Honourable the Minister of Health, sir.

HEALTH: So now it's my fault, eh? I am responsible for the flies as well?

AGRICULTURE: It is your job to bandage the Father of the Nation. Might as well complete what your puppy here started.

HEALTH: I have news for you. From now on you'll take turns to change the bandages. Never again will you see me do it.

CULTURE: How do you change them anyway? We don't have any clean bandages here.

HEALTH: Ha! Clean bandages, eh? Have you ever seen anything clean here? Use the same bandage. Just turn it around and use the other side. That's what I used to do when I was the bandage changer.

CULTURE: It has been turned around so many times, now it's hard with caked pus.

AGRICULTURE: Why don't you get the boy's shirt and use it as a bandage?

CULTURE: That wouldn't be right, would it?

He quickly rolls the filthy bandage around the President's leg.

CULTURE: There! It's all bandaged now. You don't need anybody's shirt for that. Remember, the Wise One said we shouldn't touch him because we don't know what his mission is.

AGRICULTURE: He didn't say we can't use his shirt as a bandage though. The Wise One is wise and specific. He would have said so if he didn't want us to use the boy's shirt as a bandage. Come to think of it, what right has the boy to wear nice clean clothes when the Father of the Nation is all dirty and tattered? I say let's take his clothes and give them to the Wise One to wear.

HEALTH: You have become as callous as your friend, the Minister of Justice.

CULTURE: This is wrong, is it not, Wise One? You said we shouldn't touch him, didn't you, Father of the Nation?

GENERAL: The Wise One cannot be disturbed at this time. He is in his moments of introspection.

CULTURE: Probably thinking up new edicts that he will decree.

AGRICULTURE: Then you'll have to help me, General, and get this boy's clothes for use by our leader. Strip, boy, and give us your clothes.

HEALTH: You can't do that. Surely you can't do it.

AGRICULTURE: Oh, yes, we can. Especially when you say we can't do it.

HEALTH: You will do it only to spite me then?

AGRICULTURE: You can't stand in the way of something which is beneficial to the Wise One ... if you know what's good for you. Come and help me, General. We'll have to take them by force. But make sure they don't get torn.

GENERAL: Are you sure we are allowed to do this?

AGRICULTURE: Have I ever led you astray, General?

The MINISTER OF AGRICULTURE, *followed by the* GENERAL, *pounces on the boy, who struggles valiantly on the ground. But they are too powerful for him. They strip him naked. He ashamedly runs to hide behind one of the boxes or crates.*

HEALTH: You bloody cowards? Why don't you pick on a man your own size. Two grown men mugging a little boy.

AGRICULTURE [*smiles slyly*]: He is not that little, if you know what I mean. Go take a look behind there and see for yourself.

HEALTH: I would expect this kind of behaviour from the Minister of Justice, but not from you. Okay, you are a scoundrel and a lecher ... but this ...it's something new. After this you have lost me forever.

AGRICULTURE: I never had you in the first place.

HEALTH: How do you know I was not going to relent?

CULTURE [*shocked*]: Beautiful princess!

AGRICULTURE: After what they have done to you, I wouldn't want you in any case. I don't go for leftovers.

CULTURE: Sour grapes. That's what it is.

The MINISTER OF AGRICULTURE *takes the young man's clothes to the* PRESIDENT.

AGRICULTURE: Your Excellency, Father of the Nation, through my resourcefulness, which has proved equal to that of our dearly departed, the Honourable the Minister of Works, I got you new clothes.

The PRESIDENT, *who seems to be quite drained and tired, slowly looks at the clothes.*

PRESIDENT: Those? I wouldn't be seen dead in such fancy clothes. It flies against our dress code as ministers of this benevolent government. We must pride ourselves on our formal look. Suits and ties. General! It is time for bed now.

GENERAL [*in his ringmaster voice*]: Ladies and gentlemen of the Cabinet, boys and girls, the Father of the Nation, the One and Only, the Great Leader of the People now retires to bed!

All applaud. The GENERAL *leads the way to the Shadows, closely followed by the* PRESIDENT. *The* MINISTER OF AGRICULTURE *throws the young man's clothes on the floor and follows them to the Shadows.*

AGRICULTURE: If the Wise One retires, so do I.
HEALTH: We'll miss you terribly.

We can see the three men sleeping in grotesque positions in the Shadows. They provide a dark background to our three remaining characters. The MINISTER OF CULTURE *picks up the clothes and throws them to the* YOUNG MAN *behind the box.*

YOUNG MAN: Thank you, sir.
CULTURE: He speaks!
HEALTH: Of course he speaks. Come here.

The MINISTER OF CULTURE *gets closer to her. She kisses him on the cheek.*

HEALTH: I am sorry I was mad at you.

CULTURE: I knew you were not yourself, beautiful princess. It is because of the things they did to you.

HEALTH: First they locked me up in a cell and exposed me to so much noise that I felt like I was in hell. My mind was about to crack. The noise prevents you from doing anything, and causes you to be physically ill. I was vomiting all over the place, and had convulsions. They said, 'We are not going to assault you, but if you survive this we shall be convinced that you are not human.'

CULTURE: The bastards! One day they'll pay for all this.

HEALTH: At the same time they instructed me to bang my head against the wall. This happened for hours on end. When it finally stopped I had become so conditioned to it that I had the searing wish for it to continue.

CULTURE: As you said, beautiful princess, it is our lot, we who have chosen to serve the nation. They didn't do anything physical to you, did they? Why are you limping?

HEALTH: Electric shock. They put electrodes in my private parts.

The fully dressed YOUNG MAN *emerges from behind the box.*

YOUNG MAN: Thank you for standing up for me, ma'am.

HEALTH: He tried to defend you too. But when they use the name of the Wise One, they become too powerful. No one can stop them.

YOUNG MAN: They are terrible people.

HEALTH: They mean no harm.

YOUNG MAN [*to* CULTURE]: You shouldn't let them treat you this way.

CULTURE: What can I do? The Wise One's intervention seems to favour them. And if the Wise One thinks I deserve this kind of treatment, then indeed I deserve it.

HEALTH: You see, they don't like culture, or people involved in it. I wouldn't be surprised one day if they decree to kill producers of all that is cultural, as the Minister of Justice intimated the other day.

CULTURE: They wouldn't dare.

HEALTH: Don't underestimate them, my friend. The Minister of Justice has a lot of influence around here. His word carries weight.

CULTURE: The fire-setter is just as wicked.

YOUNG MAN: Fire-setter? Who is the fire-setter?

HEALTH: The Minister of Agriculture. He used to set fires before he became a minister.

CULTURE: That's how he became a Cabinet minister.

YOUNG MAN: By setting fires:

HEALTH: You see, when the revolution was fought against the colonial settlers he opposed it, saying how could the people stand for themselves and survive without the masters. When the revolution was won by the people he was suddenly hit by the fire bug.

CULTURE: He went around starting fires, and dancing around them, and then disappeared before he was caught. Then he would boast about it, and justify his actions – sometimes even quoting from the Bible … any verse where fire was remotely mentioned.

HEALTH: He did a lot of damage, you know. He set fire to barns, and the tears of widows did not touch his conscience.

CULTURE: He set fire to crops in the fields. He set fire to houses. Fires that burned on and on, searing the soul of the community.

YOUNG MAN: And he was never caught?

HEALTH: Never. He had his lieutenants, whom he trained in the art of arson. And they were good at disappearing.

CULTURE: Then one day he received a conversion.

HEALTH: Yeah. One day he received a conversion and the fire bug left him. He saw the damage he and his lieutenants were causing the community, and regretted it.

CULTURE: He appealed to his lieutenants to stop, and was hailed as a good man, a man of peace and of conscience.

HEALTH: A man who loved the people.

CULTURE: But his lieutenants had tasted the joys of fire. They refused to stop, and continued in their orgy of fire-setting.

HEALTH: He joined the fire brigade and put the fires out.

CULTURE: He was hailed as the saviour of the people from the scourge of fire. He was awarded the highest peace prize in the land, and was showered with honours.

YOUNG MAN: This is beautiful. It's the famous old trick of starting wars, then stopping them, and winning peace prizes for it.

CULTURE: Don't think that some of us did not oppose the prize, especially because at the time I was the Minister of Agriculture, and the man had destroyed too many farms. The Cabinet insisted that he was being honoured for putting the fires out. 'But he started these fires in the first place,' I said. The Wise One, who is always so wise, convinced me when he said, 'It is not important that he started the fires. What is important is that he stopped them. We don't focus on the negative. We look for the positive.'

HEALTH: Yes. He was awarded the Noble Peace Prize by the government, presented by the Wise One himself at a big ceremony attended by world dignitaries. Because he was a Peace Prize winner he was invited to join the government.

CULTURE: The presence of a Peace Prize Laureate in our ranks enhanced the prestige of this benevolent government. What was left now was to choose a portfolio more suited to his talents.

HEALTH: 'Agriculture! Agriculture!' Shouted the Honourable the Minister of Justice.

YOUNG MAN: Why Agriculture?

CULTURE: It was decreed that since he burned crops when the fire bug hit him, he must be the Minister of Agriculture. What hurt most ... that was my ministry. I was transferred from my ministry to the newly created Ministry of Culture. All of a sudden I found myself having to oversee groups of rustics who danced for tourists at the airport or at the Market Square.

YOUNG MAN: Why did they pick you for Culture?

CULTURE: Because I compose poems.

HEALTH: Which are quite atrocious, actually.

CULTURE: Don't believe her. I have seen people being moved whenever I read them. Only my colleagues in this Cabinet are deaf to the voice of the muse.

YOUNG MAN: I am quite familiar with your poetry, sir.

CULTURE: You are?

YOUNG MAN: People outside are aware that the Honourable Minister is a poet of sorts. People say that you, in your capacity as Minister of Culture, instructed publishers to publish your work.

CULTURE: So, what do they think of my work?

YOUNG MAN: No one has read it. Once I picked up a copy of your book somewhere. I was surprised to see that your poems do have some merit, although in an old-fashioned and naïve manner.

CULTURE: Naïve? You call a Cabinet Minister of the Wise One's government naïve?

YOUNG MAN: If you decide to write you must expect critics to comment on your work. Your poems, for instance, have rhyme which is forced through inverted sentences.

HEALTH: Are you saying that they are not good at all? It's nice to hear comments from an independent critic. All the views we have about the greatness of his work are from him.

CULTURE: I don't think you should encourage our young visitor to make disrespectful comments about an esteemed colleague, beautiful princess.

HEALTH: You know he was adamant that his poems be prescribed at schools. But other honourable members influenced the Minister of Education to refuse. Do you think they should have been prescribed?

CULTURE: Beautiful princess, beautiful princess, don't talk about me like this.

YOUNG MAN: No. He does nothing in his poems but praise the wisdom of the Wise One.

CULTURE: We all praise the wisdom of the Wise One.

HEALTH: He was quite disgruntled when they were not prescribed.

CULTURE [angry and shouting]: And why should I not be disgruntled? I get the short end of the stick every time. My ministry is the only one where there are no opportunities to get kickbacks like in other ministries. Prescribing the books was the only opportunity I had to get a little something by way of royalties. In your ministry you have all the opportunities to get kickbacks from drug companies. Yet you stand there and condemn me in front of a stranger for being disgruntled when they refused to prescribe my poems. Even when the National Theatre was constructed it was the Minister of Works who got the kickbacks, whereas in all fairness I should have been paid most of since this was a building in my jurisdiction.

HEALTH: You don't have to be rude to me, you know that. I won't stand for it.

She turns away from him and concentrates all her attention on the YOUNG MAN.

CULTURE: I am sorry, beautiful princess. I did not mean to be rude.

HEALTH: Don't ever talk to me again.

CULTURE: Please, beautiful princess, don't do this to me.

HEALTH [*to the* YOUNG MAN]: Anyway, what are you doing in a dump like this? You look quite ... out of place ... quite ... beautiful.

YOUNG MAN [*embarrassed*]: Beautiful, ma'am? Please ...

HEALTH: Of course, you are a child. You have a right to be beautiful.

YOUNG MAN: I am not quite a child. In years, maybe ... but in other ways, no. [*Boastfully.*] I have seen many things.

CULTURE [*quite jealously*]: He's nothing but a child, beautiful princess. You cannot possibly have the slightest interest in someone who still smells of the milk from his mother's breasts.

The MINISTER OF HEALTH *puts her arm around the* YOUNG MAN.

HEALTH: You have seen many things, eh? Tell me about it.

CULTURE: Good night, beautiful princess. I am going to sleep now. Sweet dreams.

She ignores him.

YOUNG MAN: Yes, I have seen many things.

CULTURE: I said good night, beautiful princess. Dream of our garden, even though it is now banned. Remember our yellow garden?

YOUNG MAN: Things that the eyes of adults would not want to see.

When there is no response the MINISTER OF CULTURE *sulkily walks to the Shadows to sleep.*

HEALTH: Like what?

YOUNG MAN [*conspiratorially*]: I have seen naked women of your age and older. The Daughters of the Revolution. I have seen them dance naked at the Market Square.

HEALTH: Many people have seen that.

YOUNG MAN: Usually men run away because they do not want to go blind.

HEALTH: And you did not run away?

YOUNG MAN: I was caught by surprise. It was the time I was living in a box in the centre of town by the Market Square.

HEALTH: The man in the box! You are the man in the box! The man who wanted to sleep like a foetus. How did you come to live like that?

YOUNG MAN: You know, before that I was an artist and I had a patron. I lived in her backyard in the suburbs. I hate that place. There are no homeless people there. Okay, there is one homeless person, but he is not really homeless. Everybody feeds him, and he is fatter than those who have homes. There is no crime. Criminals prey only on the poor. No murders. Only one person was killed in the four years I lived there, and he was run down by a car. It was a dull life. A life I would not wish on my worst enemy.

HEALTH: And so you left the wealthy suburbs for the city centre, a place infested by the homeless and by all sorts of criminals?

YOUNG MAN: And there I saw the Daughters of the Revolution. I would have run away, I swear. I don't want to be blind. But I was sleeping in my box when they came, and I peeped through my peephole and saw them. They paraded naked in the town square, their bodies marred by shrapnel scars.

HEALTH: How do you live in your box?

YOUNG MAN: I maintain myself by selling flowers. Better than peddling drugs.

HEALTH: Well, you can't sell flowers any more. The Wise One has banned all flowers in the land.

YOUNG MAN: Can he really do that? That's a very stupid thing to do.

HEALTH: Never say that again! Especially in the presence of the other ministers. The Wise One is wise, and there is a good reason for everything he does.

YOUNG MAN: I am sorry, ma'am, but I think he is stupid. Any man who bans flowers cannot be smart at all. Is this the same beloved man we lined the streets for when I was a pupil at school? Yes, as school kids we lined the streets and waved little flags. He would smile his kindly smile and wave back at us. We did that all the time, you know. When he was going to inspect the fields, schools would close, and we would be there lining the streets for him. When he was going on a trip, we would be there all the way to the airport, lining the streets and waving the flags. We loved it because it meant there would be no school that day. And these trips and inspections were so frequent that in any one year we had more days lining the streets than school days. We loved him for that! Has he now turned into a tin-pot dictator who hates flowers?

HEALTH [*amused in spite of herself*]: Your harsh words about a man who has so wisely led this country are uncalled for, to say the least.

YOUNG MAN: How did you end up with people like these, anyway? You should be out there marching with the Daughters of the Revolution.

HEALTH: The Daughters of the Revolution, eh? [*She laughs.*] Once we were on the same side as them. They were part of us. They were one with us. We won the war, and soon forgot what it was we were fighting for in the first place. What the war was all about. They say they still remember. They are hoarders of ancient memories. We say we move on and talk about the present and the future. They want to talk about yesterday!

YOUNG MAN: Memory is all they have at the moment, ma'am. Now they want to add to it restitution. Only a combination of memory and restitution will speed up the process of healing their shrapnel wounds – which are still painful even though it's years since the war.

HEALTH: You said when you saw the naked women they had scars … healed scars!

YOUNG MAN: Scars … wounds … Ma'am, I tell you, they may look like scars, but inside they are bleeding wounds … dripping with the agony of freshness.

HEALTH: And your young eyes have seen all these things?

YOUNG MAN: I have seen them all, ma'am. And more. My eyes have seen many more things that I can't even tell you about.

HEALTH: And you survived it all, without blindness?

YOUNG MAN: I am here, in front of you. And I can see you clearly. My eyes itch a lot though, and sometimes they cry for no reason at all. But I count my blessings because I can see you.

HEALTH: Oh, child, what have they done to you?

YOUNG MAN: More than you'll ever guess, ma'am.

HEALTH: Don't worry. I am here. No one will ever harm you again.

She mothers him and smothers him with hugs and kisses. Lights fade to dark.

Scene Four

Lights rise on the MINISTER OF JUSTICE *who is sitting on the floor, weeping and moaning, and on the* YOUNG MAN *who is sitting on one of the boxes some distance away. He is disinterestedly looking at the* MINISTER OF JUSTICE. *The other honourable members are grotesque shadows in the Shadows. A still sleepy* MINISTER OF HEALTH *emerges from the Shadows and joins the* YOUNG MAN. *At first she does not see the* MINISTER OF JUSTICE, *who has stopped sniffling for a while.*

HEALTH: You didn't sleep?

YOUNG MAN: I never sleep at all, ma'am. Since my eyes saw things they were not supposed to see, I never sleep.

HEALTH: You need to sleep sometimes, if only to escape from the sordidness of our waking moments.

YOUNG MAN: There is no escape, ma'am. What with dreams that are more harrowing than anything we encounter in our waking moments haunting me! But it is for other reasons that I don't sleep. I am dead scared, ma'am. I am afraid that one night I'll sleep and wake up blind. I know that's bound to happen sooner or later. It happens like that, you know, when you've seen things you're not supposed to see. You sleep, in the morning you open your eyes, and you can't see a damn thing. It's like the eyelids have been glued together.

HEALTH: So you will never sleep … forever…?

YOUNG MAN: … and ever, world without end, Amen. But blindness will get tired of waiting for me to sleep, and will find a way of attacking me while I'm wide awake. I told you last night that my eyes itch, and sometimes cry for no reason at all. Anyway, as long as I can see I don't want to sleep at all. I cannot waste a single precious moment sleeping. I need to see as much of what is happening around me as possible. Then I can go blind in peace and not miss the dubious pleasures of sight.

The MINISTER OF JUSTICE *starts sniffling, and then weeping and moaning again.*

HEALTH: What was that?

YOUNG MAN: It's him [*pointing to the* MINISTER OF JUSTICE]. They brought him back in the middle of the night … or maybe it was more towards dawn.

The MINISTER OF HEALTH *walks to him and looks at him closely. He is a haggard figure, bruised all over.*

HEALTH: Wow! They gave him the works, didn't they now?

YOUNG MAN: He's been crying for hours, non-stop.

The MINISTER OF CULTURE *joins them*

HEALTH: And we thought he would be the strongest of us all.

CULTURE: Strongest? He confessed that he was so scared that he peed on himself!

HEALTH: No!

CULTURE: Oh, yes, he did. When they'd taken you away, he did.

JUSTICE: To hell with being strong. It was a night of hell. And all because of you or you.

HEALTH & CULTURE: Us? Why us?

JUSTICE: We have been sold out. The cause has been betrayed. Who else would be responsible if not one of you two?

HEALTH: There are others here, you know. There's the General and there is the Minister of Agriculture!

JUSTICE: It can't be the General. He is too close to the Wise One to do that kind of thing.

YOUNG MAN: How do you know? He just sits there quietly and says nothing. Still waters run deep.

CULTURE: Do you really think it is the General? Why would he do a thing like that? What does he have against us, or against his own mentor, the Wise One?

YOUNG MAN: You just can't trust anyone these days.

HEALTH: And what about the Minister of Agriculture? How is he above suspicion in your eyes?

JUSTICE: He's an honourable man!

YOUNG MAN: He used to set fires. He's capable of betraying your cause, whatever it is!

JUSTICE: You told him about the fires! You ratted to a strange boy on an esteemed colleague? I was right. You two are the traitors. We have suffered all this pain and humiliation because of you! [*Cries again.*]

HEALTH: Oh, grow up. I had nothing to do with it.

CULTURE: I have suffered as well. I had nothing to do with it. Where is he, anyway, your friend, the Minister of Agriculture?

JUSTICE [*crying*]: They took him away!

YOUNG MAN: I saw it all. After they threw him [*indicating the MINISTER OF JUSTICE*] in here, the shadowy figure just stood at the door. I could see that it was focusing its attention at the Shadows, particularly at the sleeping figure of your fire-setting friend.

JUSTICE: Don't call him that.

YOUNG MAN: And the fire-setter just stood up, and like a sleepwalker he emerged from the Shadows, and went straight for the door. The shadowy figure seized him. He uttered a bloodcurdling scream. The door was slammed behind them. And then the chains and the keys. It was a wonderful sight to behold.

JUSTICE: I hope they won't do to him what they told me they did to the Honourable Minister of Works.

HEALTH: What a guy! They told you about him too, then?

JUSTICE: So you knew about it all along? You knew that he died a most ignominious death, and you said nothing about it.

HEALTH: I learnt of it the same way you did. In the course of torture and humiliation they said if I didn't confess and betray the cause, I was going to die as ignominiously as the Minister of Works. Then they described his death in all its gory detail. I didn't want to talk about it. I wanted to remember him the way he used to be, a great guy. What a guy!

JUSTICE [panics]: We are all going to die. They are going to kill us all, except for the traitor, of course. They told me that I am next. They said I must go and think about it. [Crying.] I don't want to die!

CULTURE: You see! That's how my cockroach felt. It didn't want to die either.

YOUNG MAN: You had a cockroach?

CULTURE: Yes. It was my pet, and he killed it.

YOUNG MAN: Why did he do that?

CULTURE: Just for the joy of it. They've always been jealous that I had a pet which kept me company. He cut its head off.

YOUNG MAN: That's cruel.

CULTURE: Still it defied him. It lived for ten days without its head. Through divine intervention it was able to live all those days.

JUSTICE: Nonsense. The Honourable the Minster of Agriculture told us that there was nothing divine about it. He is a scientific man. He explained to us the pest was able to live that long without its head because it has no central nervous system. It died of hunger because our man of culture could not feed it.

CULTURE: You have no remorse at all. I wish they would keep their promise and kill you too.

JUSTICE: Did you hear what he said? For sure he is the traitor. Otherwise how can he say such things if he has no dealings with our torturers?

HEALTH: He is hurt about his pet, don't you understand that?

JUSTICE: But it happened so long ago.

HEALTH: You don't forget a pet that easily. I still have not forgotten my spider.

CULTURE [*smiles fondly*]: Ah, the black widow spider!

YOUNG MAN: He killed your pet too? He's been busy, hey!

JUSTICE: No. Not the spider. I had nothing to do with the death of her spider.

HEALTH: They were beautiful, those spiders. A huge black widow female and a small male. They mated, and then the female ate the male. Wouldn't it be nice if things happened like that with human beings as well?

JUSTICE: Ha! Women eating their men after love making!

HEALTH: The age of the disposable male is coming, my friend. It is surely coming. It's going to happen one day when the human species has evolved to the great levels of the black widow.

CULTURE: I was there. I saw the grin on its face. I knew it had eaten its mate

YOUNG MAN: That's beautiful, I say. It is more of such beauty that I want to see before I peacefully go blind. What happened to her … the black widow, I mean?

HEALTH: She disappeared. And of course we know who we suspect for her disappearance.

JUSTICE: I swear it was not me.

HEALTH: We know who it was who threatened to eat her when we had not been fed for many days.

JUSTICE: But I was only joking!

HEALTH: We know who said, 'She eats males, eh? I'll show her that males know how to eat too.'

JUSTICE: I didn't mean it. I did not eat your spider.

YOUNG MAN: What a collection you have here. Spider eaters and fire setters. And now he is afraid to die. Maybe he is the traitor. Has it not occurred to you that he is such a coward that he could easily rat on his friends to save his skin?

JUSTICE: Who is this boy who is accusing me of being a traitor? How can I suffer like this and be a traitor?

The PRESIDENT, *led by the* GENERAL *in his circus ringmaster persona, emerge from the Shadows.*

GENERAL: Ladies and gentlemen of the Cabinet! Boys and Girls! The One and Only, the Supreme Commander, His Excellency the Wise One, Father of the Nation, Mr … President!

All applaud mechanically, except for the YOUNG MAN *who looks on with amusement. The* PRESIDENT *takes a bow, and smiles benevolently at each of them. The* YOUNG MAN *bursts out laughing. He quickly keeps quiet when they all glare at him disapprovingly.*

JUSTICE: Your Excellency! Something must be done, otherwise we're all going to die. Do something to save us, Father of the Nation.

PRESIDENT: Are you beginning to snap? Be strong, man. You are a member of the Wise One's benevolent government. Stand straight. Be proud and strong.

HEALTH: How long can we continue to be strong, Wise One? How long can we continue to be unbreakable? We have been sold out by one of us, Your Excellency. We have been betrayed. The sky is falling on our heads.

PRESIDENT [*a flash of anger*]: You fool, how can the sky fall? Have we not contained greater threats before? Have we not consistently triumphed over those bent on destroying us? Have we not stopped a thousand skies from falling on our heads?

JUSTICE: Forgive us, Your Excellency. It is difficult to stay strong when we cannot trust one another.

HEALTH: And the Daughters of the Revolution on the other hand are getting bolder and bolder. They are bent on shaming us to our destruction. They are closing in on us.

PRESIDENT: We are closing in on them. The Sodom and Gomorrah that they are creating in the streets ... and at the Market Square of all places ... is going to stop.

HEALTH: The Wise One has spoken!

JUSTICE: It is going to stop!

PRESIDENT: We know about their plans for a beauty contest. We are going to nip it in the bud. I am going to make a very important decree. Now the government must control and regulate beauty contests. Of course we'll not say we are doing it to stop the Daughters of the Revolution. They must not think that we enact legislation especially for them, otherwise they'll get big-headed.

YOUNG MAN [*softly to* HEALTH]: Too late. They have already held their beauty contest.

PRESIDENT: What's the boy saying?

HEALTH [*panicking*]: He says the Daughters of the Revolution have held the beauty contest already.

Everyone is struck with fear at the news.

PRESIDENT: What! When? How is that possible? Did you see it? Does the populace know about this?

JUSTICE: I don't think we should worry about the populace. Most people regard the Daughters of the Revolution as mad women. They stand on the sides of the road and laugh at them.

YOUNG MAN: Not any more. People take them quite seriously. And yes, I saw the beauty contest. It is one of the things my eyes were not supposed to see. Men fled.

PRESIDENT: And you did not flee?

YOUNG MAN: I could not flee. It was early in the morning, and the streets were teeming with people going to work. I was sleeping in my box, when I was woken up by some commotion outside. I peeped, and saw men fleeing for their lives. I knew that the Daughters of the Revolution were up to something. At first I thought it was their usual naked march. But no, they were holding a beauty contest, where one of the categories that were being judged was the number and extent of shrapnel scars on their naked bodies.

CULTURE: Who won?

PRESIDENT: Does it matter who won? What matters is that they held the beauty contest under our noses, even though we thought we were quite vigilant.

YOUNG MAN: I'll tell you who won. An old old woman. She was very graceful, and she carried her scars with such pride I could have kissed her. I heard them say that her good-for-nothing son is a Cabinet minister.

They all look at the MINISTER OF JUSTICE, *who hides his face in shame.*

ALL: Your mother!

YOUNG MAN: Oh, so that's the spider eater's mother? Man, your mother is a beauty. How did you turn out like this?

JUSTICE: You call me that again I'll…

YOUNG MAN: You'll what? Eh, spider eater? You'll what?

JUSTICE: Just don't call me that, okay?

PRESIDENT: We must be slipping. General, how did this beauty contest happen under our noses?

GENERAL: They took us by surprise, sir. It was an ambush.

HEALTH: It was a blow. They have given us a blow from which we may never recover.

JUSTICE: Yes. The populace now knows that they have triumphed over us. They will lose all respect for us.

PRESIDENT: There is no satisfying these Daughters of the Revolution. We gave them symbols. Still they complain. Great symbols! Flags! Anthems! Street names! All changed to reflect the new order of freedom. But are they happy? No! They want more! What do they want? I'll tell you what they want. They want our blood. They want our heads on a platter.

YOUNG MAN: They have tried to eat symbols, but they still remain hungry.

PRESIDENT: And what do we eat, eh? Do they know what we eat? Do they know we have to grovel for our food like dogs? Do they know that sometimes they forget to feed us, and we have to eat our own lice? Do they think it's a banquet to be a government minister?

JUSTICE: I know what we can do to offset the impact of the beauty contest. Let's enhance the image of the Wise One.

CULTURE: The Wise One is already great and wonderful. How do you enhance him?

YOUNG MAN [*sarcastically*]: Yeah. How do you improve on perfection?

JUSTICE: The Wise One is already perfect, thank God.

HEALTH: Although the populace seem not to be aware of that.

JUSTICE: Exactly. That is why we must enhance his image, not him. And we can do that by giving him a new title.

YOUNG MAN [*laughing*]: He already has a string of unnecessary titles as far as I'm concerned.

JUSTICE: Who asked you? You are not even a member of this Cabinet.

CULTURE: I can think of an excellent title. The Anointed One. Let us call him the Anointed One.

JUSTICE: I think the Chosen One sounds much better.

HEALTH: You don't like the Anointed One because it comes from the Honourable the Minister of Culture. Well, I go with the Anointed One.

CULTURE: Thank you, beautiful princess.

YOUNG MAN: Chosen and anointed by whom?

JUSTICE: Anyway I think both titles undermine His Excellency's natural wisdom and attribute it to some supernatural being.

CULTURE: But I feel that titles which hint at a divine hand in the Wise One's actions will get us more following even from those who regard themselves as born-again believers who have chosen to divorce themselves from the things of the world.

PRESIDENT: Why don't you use both titles and get it over with?

GENERAL: The Wise One has spoken.

OTHERS: It shall be so.

CULTURE: I propose that in addition to the divine titles, the picture of the Wise One must be on the front page of all newspapers always till the end of time.

HEALTH: Great idea!

JUSTICE: Another proposal. The titles of Chosen One and Anointed One will certainly get us a following from the believers. We need another title to get intellectuals in our houses of learning on our side. Students are becoming restless too.

HEALTH: I know! Let us call him Doctor!

CULTURE: Yes, indeed! Whoever heard of such a great man being called plain Mister?

YOUNG MAN: Don't you have to get a PhD to be called a doctor?

JUSTICE: We'll award him one right away.

CULTURE: Who's going to do it? The Honourable the Minister of Education is not here.

HEALTH: You can do it. Your ministry is closest to his.

JUSTICE: You can't give such great responsibility to him.

CULTURE: And why not?

YOUNG MAN: Yes. Why not?

JUSTICE: Okay. Just do it then.

CULTURE: Wise One, Father of the Nation, you who is the Anointed One and the Chosen One, allow me to put my hand on your head.

The PRESIDENT *bows down, and The* MINISTER OF CULTURE *puts his hand on his head.*

CULTURE: Wise One, Father of the Nation, by the powers vested in me by this Honourable Cabinet, I hereby confer on you the degree of Doctor of Philosophy.

YOUNG MAN: You may kiss the bride.

JUSTICE: He is a fly in our ointment, isn't he?

YOUNG MAN: Sorry. I just thought I should also get into the spirit of things.

JUSTICE: General, remember that from now on when you introduce the Wise One you don't say, 'Mr ... President!' but 'Dr ... President!'

GENERAL [*in his ringmaster voice*]: Ladies and gentlemen of the Cabinet! Boys and girls! Here's the Supreme Commander, the One and Only, The Anointed One, hey the Chosen One, His Excellency the Wise One, Father of the Nation, Dr ... President!

All except the young man give their mechanical applause. The PRESIDENT *smiles benevolently, and takes triumphal bows.*

JUSTICE: I'll tell you what we need now. We need a new portrait of the Wise One to show his new academic self. Get a good painter. Then print many reproductions. In their homes, because of their love for the Wise One, the populace will have his portrait on their walls. And no picture must be hung higher than the Wise One's.

They all look at the MINISTER OF CULTURE.

CULTURE: No. Don't look at me. I told you that I am not getting artists any more.

JUSTICE: It is your job as Minister of Culture.

CULTURE: They won't talk to me since the incident with the last artist who used to create masterpieces of this Honourable Cabinet. Some want to be paid upfront.

YOUNG MAN: And so they should. Especially after you robbed me of my livelihood.

JUSTICE: Robbed you? Who robbed you?

YOUNG MAN: You all did. You and your President.

JUSTICE: Our President. Don't be disrespectful. He is the President of the whole country.

YOUNG MAN: I am sure you'd make him President of the whole universe if you had the power. But you are all a bunch of thieves, I say.

JUSTICE: Wise One, do you hear what he calls us? I propose we ask the General to give him the works.

PRESIDENT [*smiles benevolently*]: We can tolerate his misguided words because we are benevolent. Your are a fortunate young man. Since we adopted the National Policy of Benevolence we have learnt to be calm and patient. There was a time when an impertinent boy like this one would have regretted that he was born. Once I sneezed and a Cabinet member forgot to say, 'Bless you!' So I blew his head off with a shot gun. You are lucky these are my benevolent days.

CULTURE: What is the young man so hot under the collar about, anyway? What did we do to him?

YOUNG MAN: What did you do to me? Are your memories so short? Am I not the artist who painted your portraits day in and day out? And what did I get for it? Scorn!

HEALTH: He is the artist!

CULTURE: I knew his face looked familiar!

JUSTICE: He did not die after all!

PRESIDENT: What does he want now? What do you want from us?

YOUNG MAN [*to* CULTURE]: You betrayed me.

CULTURE: I was betrayed by my colleagues. I pleaded with them. But they refused to pay.

YOUNG MAN: Then you came back to me, and asked me to paint the sets for you because the Pope was coming. I said no, pay me first for the paintings of the Cabinet. You promised that you would talk with your colleagues and everything would be all right. I painted the most beautiful houses on those sets, and the most beautiful smiling faces. But still I got nothing. You lied to me.

PRESIDENT: What does he mean he got nothing? Didn't he get the papers that I signed myself, and that were countersigned by the Honourable the Minister of Culture – the papers that honoured him as a great artist of the people. What more payment did he want?

The YOUNG MAN *takes many pieces of paper from his pockets and throws them on the floor.*

YOUNG MAN: There! These are the slips of paper with which you paid me. They don't mean a damn thing. Just some stupid honour for serving my country.

PRESIDENT: Where is your patriotism? You are not proud of serving your country?

YOUNG MAN: The hell I am. Was I supposed to eat these pieces of paper. I spent hours, days, months … painting your stupid grins. And what did I get for it, eh?

CULTURE: Calm down, man. I am sure we can still settle this.

YOUNG MAN: You know how many stupid pieces of paper I have here? More than a hundred. After each painting you gave me one slip of paper. I did dozens of paintings. Then you decided that the new image that you were cultivating was that of benevolence. All the paintings were recalled wherever they were, and I was instructed to paint smiles on your faces. More slips of paper.

JUSTICE: You can't blame us for that. It was essential to have a smiling Cabinet in the spirit of the new policy. Previously only the Wise One had a smile because he had the monopoly on benevolence. Once he had agreed to share benevolence with the rest of the Cabinet old paintings had to be changed accordingly.

PRESIDENT: Was I not informed that the young artist had died? How did he resurrect himself?

YOUNG MAN: Ha! You thought I was dead, didn't you? When I began to bother you demanding that the pieces of paper be converted into cash since I couldn't eat them, you set your guards on me.

PRESIDENT: You were supposed to frame them, young man, and put them on all your walls. Those were important papers. They had my signature on them.

JUSTICE: The guards came back and reported that you fell off a cliff.

YOUNG MAN: That's what they thought. I hid myself. I was in hiding for a long time.

HEALTH: We all believed that you were dead. Even your mother.

YOUNG MAN: Oh, my mother! They called her a mad woman because she demanded my body. She said, 'He is my son. His body belongs to me. Now that you have murdered him, give me the body of my son!'

JUSTICE: You can't blame us for that too. You should have informed your mother that you were alive. Now, you see, she was a mad woman. She danced at the Market Square, throwing stones at passing vehicles, and demanding the return of her son or of his corpse. You should have told her you were not dead!

YOUNG MAN: And expose myself to you? I see what you are trying to do. You are trying to blame me for my mother's death? That won't do, my friend. You bloody well know that you killed my mother. You have your mother, and she is a beauty queen. Mine is dead, gone forever.

JUSTICE: Mine is as good as dead too. She is a traitor who has thrown in her lot with the mad women.

YOUNG MAN: My mother didn't deserve to die like that.

PRESIDENT: How did she die?

JUSTICE: We hanged her for dancing for the Daughters of the Revolution, sir. It was your decree.

PRESIDENT: Oh, yes, we did, didn't we?

YOUNG MAN: She never danced for them. It just so happened that she was dancing at the Market Square and they were marching at the same time. The Daughters of the Revolution stopped and watched, and shouted , 'Go, sister! Go! Go! Go, sister!' They had for a moment forgotten about their demonstration and were overwhelmed by the dance.

The YOUNG MAN *dances a very frenzied dance, shouting 'Go, sister! Go!' The Honourable Members cannot help but clap their hands to the rhythm. When he finally stops he is breathless.*

YOUNG MAN: And you know what happened after that? At night your people came and picked her up and hanged her for the crime of entertaining the Daughters of the Revolution.

HEALTH: I am sorry we caused you so much grief.

CULTURE: Me too, beautiful princess. Include me in your sorrow.

YOUNG MAN [*bubbling with enthusiasm*]: My mother! She always danced so beautifully. I do not know … I do not understand why it is dance that moves me more than anything else. Yes. Dance. And dance. It makes me cry … It need not be a sad dance to make me cry … The most joyous dance fills my eyes with tears. Even more than any song will ever do. And beautiful songs move me too. But not as much as dance. I have filled buckets with my salty tears when watching a dance movement executed by experts. To me a dancer is a god. Or better still, a goddess.

The MINISTER OF HEALTH *is so moved that she rushes to the* YOUNG MAN, *and mothers him, smothering him with hugs and kisses.*

PRESIDENT: Let's not be carried away now. Sometimes painful decisions have to be made for the good of the state. When we killed your mother we were not really killing her as a person. We were killing the idea. As much as her memory lives in your minds it lives in ours too. We had nothing against her personally. It really was nothing personal. If you ask me, we all love her right up to this day.

YOUNG MAN: What did you achieve by her death? The Daughters of the Revolution are still there more powerful than ever. They are closing in, and they are going to cut off your balls.

All facially and gesturally express shock at such language directed at the President.

JUSTICE [*to* HEALTH]: You see what happens when you encourage him with your cheap kisses.

HEALTH: Oh, he's just overwrought. He means no harm.

YOUNG MAN: Oh, yes. The Daughters of the Revolution are geared for one final act of defiance that will destroy you forever!

JUSTICE: He knows something that we do not know.

PRESIDENT: What are they planning now?

YOUNG MAN: After the success of their beauty contest they now plan to perform the whole pitiki theatre of rebirth, including ditolobonya dance, in public, at the Market Square, in full view of everyone ... of men of children ...

JUSTICE: What's the big deal? I have seen little girls in grass skirts perform ditolobonya for tourists.

PRESIDENT: That is a watered down version that little girls do for fun. The pitiki theatre of rebirth is serious business.

JUSTICE: What are the implications of this form of protest?

PRESIDENT: Catastrophe! That's what it means. The pitiki theatre of rebirth, with its ditolobonya dance, is a very secret performance that is done by women only for a women only audience. A public performance will bring catastrophe to the land. We've got to stop them at all costs.

YOUNG MAN: When you failed to stop the beauty contest?

JUSTICE: Oh, my God, we are doomed.

PRESIDENT: Don't panic … don't panic! We've got to work out something. Damn those Daughters of the damn Revolution! Damn them!

HEALTH [*to the* YOUNG MAN]: Can't you help us stop this madness?

CULTURE: Yes, please do. It is for the good of the country to stop the performance.

PRESIDENT: Enlist the young man. After all his mother was a mad dancer. He can speak the same language as the other mad women. They will believe in him, and will have confidence in him. The young man must be used to foil the theatre of rebirth. It is the least he can do for his country.

YOUNG MAN: After what you did to me? Why would I want to help you? Do you really understand what you have done to me?

HEALTH: Yes, we do. And like I said, no one will ever harm you again. We are very very sorry.

JUSTICE: Speak for yourself. I cannot be sorry for any wise decision made by the Wise One.

PRESIDENT: There might be need to be sorry, even though when the decision was made it was wise. It was the truth of the day. Who can say it's still true today?

JUSTICE: If the Wise One says so. I am sorry too.

YOUNG MAN: After my mother was hanged, I sat for days on end at the Market Square selling forgiveness. I had seen buskers playing their violins and their flutes, selling their songs. It occurred to me that I had something to sell too. Forgiveness. But there were not enough takers.

JUSTICE: Forgive them for what?

YOUNG MAN: For what happened to me, and to my mother. They were there. They witnessed the whole thing. But they said nothing. They did nothing. I would let go of my anger only if they bought my forgiveness. There were no takers. I didn't see you there. You claim now that you are sorry, but I didn't see you there buying my forgiveness. My forgiveness is not cheap, ma'am. Not enough people came to pay for it. As a result I am still seething. No, ma'am I can't help you. As a matter of fact I plan to do an agitation of my own at the Market Square.

PRESIDENT: You are going to rabble-rouse too? Nobody is going to pay any attention to you, my boy. The Market Square rabble are only interested in slitting each other's throats.

YOUNG MAN: That's exactly what I am going to tell them. When the ruling classes disagree they don't kill one another. They joke about their disagreements at cocktail parties, while we murder each other about those very disagreements. This is a war that is fought in boardrooms, and the common men and women are the foot soldiers who must make the ultimate sacrifice.

HEALTH: You are a great painter. Why don't you stick to what you do best, and forget vengeance?

YOUNG MAN: Painting, eh? [*Laughs mockingly.*] When no one came to buy my forgiveness, I tried to paint my robbers and my mother's killers to their destruction. I tried to paint them out of existence … to paint their deaths and the resurrection of those they had destroyed. But they were too strong. They survived my paintings. Now I have to supplement painting with other methods. Hence my agitations, or rabble-rousing as you choose to call it.

CULTURE: I propose we help this young man. Let us buy him paints and brushes. Let us fill his house with art materials of all sorts.

JUSTICE: Why would we want to do that when he wants to destroy us?

CULTURE: To keep his mind on his art, so that he may forget about his agitations.

PRESIDENT: Brilliant. It is not usual to hear such brilliance from the man of culture.

CULTURE: Thank you, Your Excellency. You are so wise.

YOUNG MAN: I have no house. I live in a box.

JUSTICE: All the better. It will be cheaper for us to fill your box with art materials than a whole house.

HEALTH: I am sorry to burst your bubble, gentlemen. But you forget that it is the policy of this benevolent government that culture is not a priority in the development of the country. In fact it is not on the agenda at all. You cannot use government funds to buy materials that will produce cultural products.

YOUNG MAN: It is not on the agenda? Who made such a foolish policy?

JUSTICE: The Wise One made the decree, and it is very foolish to call him foolish.

YOUNG MAN: I don't care who made the decree. It is a foolish decree. Are you so deaf that you have not heard the message of the Dausi?

CULTURE: What is that?

YOUNG MAN: The message of the Diaru, the bards of ancient Soninke civilisations of West Africa many centuries ago. The Dausi is an epic composed by the Diaru, about the rise and fall of fabulously rich African empires.

PRESIDENT: The young man must explain himself for the benefit of the members of my benevolent Cabinet, who may not understand what he is driving at.

YOUNG MAN:

All creatures die, be buried, and vanish.

Kings and heroes die, are buried, and vanish.

I, too, shall die, shall be buried, and vanish.

But the Dausi,

The song of my battles,

Shall not die.

It shall be sung again and again.

It shall outlive all kings and heroes.

Hoooh! That I might do such deeds! Hoooh! that I might sing the Dausi!

Wagadu will be lost,

But the Dausi shall endure and live!

The Honourable Members *seem to be dumbfounded. Obviously they don't understand what he is talking about. He laughs mockingly at them.*

YOUNG MAN: And I tell you, Honourable Members of this foolish Cabinet, Wagadu – the homeland of the great Soninke – was lost and recovered and lost many times. But the Dausi endured. That is why I am able to quote from it today. Governments shall come and go. Empires shall rise and fall. Even civilisations shall come to pass. But art is forever. It lives beyond politicians, beyond governments, beyond empires, even beyond civilisations.

PRESIDENT: Perhaps we should call you for formal hearings where you can argue your case. We are benevolent. Benevolence means flexibility. Obviously you feel very strongly about this matter. We'll give you a fair hearing. But now we have urgent problems. Our immediate problem is: how do we stop the Daughters of the Revolution from performing the theatre of rebirth, the secret pitiki theatre, in broad daylight at the Market Square?

CULTURE: If only we know what this pitiki involves, and how it is done.

PRESIDENT: Knowing or not knowing will not help us in any way. It is enough to know that a public performance of pitiki and its ditolobonya dance means disaster. In any case there is no way we can know. Only women know.

JUSTICE [indicating HEALTH]: She is a woman, is she not ... or at least claims to be one.

HEALTH: I do not know anything about pitiki. I never had children. Only women who have experienced giving birth are allowed into the room where the performances are held.

YOUNG MAN: I know. I have seen the theatre of rebirth.

HEALTH: That is a lie! No man has seen the pitiki theatre.

YOUNG MAN: Oh, yes, I did. It is one of the things my eyes were not supposed to see.

They all crowd around him.

CULTURE: Tell us about it ... please!

YOUNG MAN: You know, even when my mother was alive ... before you killed her ... I loved to sleep in a box. The small box made me sleep in a foetal position, which I found very relaxing. Our home was only one room and my box stayed in the corner, at the foot of my mother's bed. So, one day I was sleeping in my box when the women came and began to perform. You know, this kind of theatre is performed to welcome a new baby into the world. They were welcoming my aunt's baby who was staying with us.

JUSTICE: The dance, boy! The dance! Spare us the details about your relatives.

YOUNG MAN: I'll just shut up if you adopt that kind of attitude, spider-eater.

JUSTICE: Okay, okay, I am sorry. But I still think that you are lying. You never saw the theatre of rebirth. You just want to appear important and superior ... that you know something that even the mighty rulers of this land do not know.

HEALTH: Never mind him. Tell us about it.

YOUNG MAN: I was sleeping in my box. They didn't know I was there. First there was the single drum. [*He makes the sound of the drum.*] And my aunt, naked as the day she was born, lay on a blanket on the floor.

HEALTH: And you saw that?

YOUNG MAN: With my two eyes. Well, one eye, since I had to peep through the hole in my box. The women of the village came, all naked, and led by my mother, in the fast fast gyration of ditolobonya dance. They danced around my aunt, who was enacting the orgasmic moment that led to the conception of the child. And then the pains of labour. And then the birth. At this point the frenzy of ditolobonya reached a peak. And the song deafened the ears. My aunt was on the floor, groaning and moaning, rolling the baby who was being welcomed into the world on her stomach.

PRESIDENT: Stop, boy! I think we have heard enough. It is obvious why men are not allowed to witness the pitiki performance. It is clear what catastrophe will befall this land if we do not stop this dance.

JUSTICE: Men will flee as they usually do when these mad women march. They will not see the theatre of rebirth and we'll be saved.

PRESIDENT: You cannot bank on that. There will be children. There will be women who have never given birth before and therefore have no right to see this performance. There'll be some foolish men whose curiosity will get the better of them. Even if there is no audience at all the catastrophe will not spare us. The dance is taboo at a public place, whether there's an audience or not. We'll not be saved! We'll not be saved! General, General, what happened to our plans to mow these mad women down with our machine guns?

GENERAL: They are crafty, sir. They have seen through us. Our guns are useless on them. Like all the men of the land our soldiers flee when these women march naked.

CULTURE: I have never seen the Wise One so distraught. It means we are really in danger.

HEALTH: Help us, young man. Please help us?

JUSTICE: Save us, young man.

YOUNG MAN: Ha! Even the spider-eater!

JUSTICE: We'll do anything you want. Only save us from the wrath of the Daughters of the Revolution!

PRESIDENT: There is anger. There is frustration. We must take it out on the lice that feed on us.

ALL: Yes, Wise One, Father of the Nation, we need the ceremonial killing of the lice to calm our spirits and diffuse our anger.

PRESIDENT: Let's take it out on the lice then! Sing the ceremonial song and crush them, ladies and gentlemen of the Cabinet.

The MINISTER OF CULTURE *starts a song, and they all sing, except the* YOUNG MAN *who seems to be amazed and amused by what is happening. This is a very monotonous song which is quite repetitive. At the same time they all take off all their clothes above the waist. They sit on the crates and boxes on different planes. They hunt for lice in the hems and seams of their shirts, jackets and so on, and when they find them they crush them with their thumbnails.*

ALL [*singing*]:
Eaters of yesterday
Are eaters of today
Masterful of change
They chew with both jaws

All freeze when they hear the chains and the keys. The door opens. The menacing figure. The MINISTER OF AGRICULTURE *is thrown into the cell. The figure disappears and the door closes. The chains and the keys. The* MINISTER OF AGRICULTURE *is dazed for a moment. Then he stands up, looks at each of the inmates, spots the* MINISTER OF CULTURE *on one of the boxes, and leaps at him. He misses him with a blow, and another one. The* MINISTER OF CULTURE *manages to escape. The* MINISTER OF AGRICULTURE *chases him around the boxes. He is obviously in pain, and runs with a terrible limp. The* YOUNG MAN *gets hold of the* MINISTER OF AGRICULTURE *who struggles to free himself from his grip. Others join in and try to stop the commotion.*

AGRICULTURE: Let me free. Let me kill this son of a bitch.

CULTURE: Why? What have I done?

HEALTH: They tortured you and humiliated you, but you have no right to pick on the Honourable the Minister of Culture!

AGRICULTURE: He is the traitor! He's the one who betrayed the cause.

JUSTICE: I thought as much. I never trusted the dweeb.

AGRICULTURE: We have suffered all this pain and humiliation because of him.

CULTURE: I am not a traitor. Tell them, beautiful princess. I cannot be the traitor.

YOUNG MAN: How do you know he is the traitor?

AGRICULTURE: As they were torturing me they let it slip that he is the one who has betrayed us from day one.

JUSTICE: Let's rip the dweeb apart.

CULTURE: Wise One! General! Help me! Please!

PRESIDENT: There is nothing we can do. Not if you betrayed your own comrades.

CULTURE: Beautiful princess, tell them that I am innocent.

HEALTH: You all saw the Honourable Minister of Culture coming in with wounds and definite signs of torture. They would not do the things they did to him if he was their spy.

AGRICULTURE: How do you know those wounds were not painted on him? How do you know they were not make-up effects as they do in the movies? Remember, he is a culture person and he knows about these things.

JUSTICE: Yes. We can't be cheated by movie special effects. We are well versed in that kind of thing. We used them too when the Pope was here.

PRESIDENT: He is a traitor. He must suffer the consequences of his actions against his own esteemed colleagues.

AGRICULTURE: The Wise One has spoken.

JUSTICE: It shall be so.

YOUNG MAN: Is that how rulers of the land administer justice? Do you condemn one of your own without even a trial?

JUSTICE: Justice is my portfolio. You have no right to talk about it. Nor to question the Wise One's decision.

AGRICULTURE: Why should we answer to this boy?

YOUNG MAN: Hold your horses, fire-setter.

AGRICULTURE: Who told this boy about the fires?

YOUNG MAN: You say they let it slip that the Minister of Culture is the spy. How do you know that they were not doing that purposely ... in order to turn you against him? It might be the old divide and rule tactic.

PRESIDENT: They are not that smart.

YOUNG MAN: Then how did they manage to keep you here for all these years. Of course they are smart. They're much too smart for you. Does this man look like a traitor to you? Okay, he's just a worm, but is he a traitor? I say, no! They don't usually choose worms to be spies, for they know that the worm is the first one you'd suspect.

HEALTH: There is sense in what the young man says.

CULTURE [*relieved*]: Oh, thank you, young man. Thank you.

JUSTICE: I still don't buy it. If the dweeb is not the traitor, then who has been betraying us?

AGRICULTURE: Yes. Who has been betraying us, son of a bitch?

CULTURE: Honest, I don't know.

YOUNG MAN: I'll tell you who has been betraying you.

HEALTH: You? How do you know?

YOUNG MAN: I don't! At least not yet. But we'll find out. When they select a spy they want someone you would never suspect. So who is above suspicion here? Ha? What about the General? Why has the General never been called for torture and humiliation?

AGRICULTURE: The General! No, I cannot believe it.

HEALTH: I would also like to know why the General has never been called for torture. Why?

AGRICULTURE: General, are you the spy?

GENERAL: Your Excellency, I cannot stand here and listen to people dirty my name.

PRESIDENT: Answer, General. Are you the traitor?

GENERAL: No. I am not.

YOUNG MAN: Could it really be the General? What does the General know that would be useful to them? Has he got a Cabinet portfolio that puts him in charge of state secrets? Do you, General?

GENERAL: Actually sometimes I would like to be given more Cabinet responsibility than just to implement decrees.

PRESIDENT: You ungrateful wretch! I made you. I can break you.

YOUNG MAN: Ah, so you see, the General is not good spy material. He's just a pawn. He merely implements your decisions. The traitor must have deep inside information to cause the damage that has been caused to you.

HEALTH: If the General is not the traitor, then who is?

YOUNG MAN: You have not answered my question yet. Who is above suspicion? Why, His Excellency the President, of course.

AGRICULTURE [*laughs sarcastically*]: The Father of the Nation cannot spy on his own government.

YOUNG MAN: Have you not asked yourself why he has never been called for his dose of torture and humiliation?

PRESIDENT: Everyone accepts that I am not capable of spying on my own government. Why should you be so bloody-minded about it?

YOUNG MAN: Why have you not been tortured like the others?

JUSTICE: Well, because he's the Father of the Nation.

HEALTH: We have always dreaded the day he would be called. We knew that would be the end of us.

YOUNG MAN: Have you not asked yourself why he stands his ground and shows no fear when the door opens?

JUSTICE: Because he is the Wise One. He is fearless.

YOUNG MAN: These torturers don't give a damn who is the Wise One and who is not. They have no reverence for any of you and your leaders. He would have been the most tortured and humiliated if he was not their man.

PRESIDENT: General! Seize this boy!

HEALTH: No, General! I think the Wise One owes us an explanation.

PRESIDENT: Explanation? I don't own anyone an explanation. I am the Wise One, the Anointed One, the Chosen One, and I can do anything I like.

YOUNG MAN: Including selling out people who have stood by you all these years. What did they promise you, Mr President?

PRESIDENT: Dr President to you. And I am not answering any questions.

YOUNG MAN: You see what I told you? This is your man. Do what you like with him.

JUSTICE: Can it really be true?

AGRICULTURE: I don't believe it.

YOUNG MAN: Ask him. Ask him to deny it. Come on Mr President. Deny that you are the traitor. General, seize him!

The GENERAL hesitates. Everyone is scared.

YOUNG MAN: Why are you so afraid of him? He's so weak ... so small and frail ...

HEALTH: Oh, Wise One, why did you do this to us when we loved you so much?

PRESIDENT: I did it for the good of the nation. You, Honourable Members, must be proud that you have suffered pain and humiliation for your people.

HEALTH: That won't fly with me, Mr President. It was for your own good. It was your way of escaping pain and humiliation at our expense. We who served you so faithfully and with so much dedication. General, seize him!

The GENERAL *seizes him. He ties his hands behind him with his necktie and puts him on one of the boxes. He stands there, half naked, a lonely figure surrounded by angry people. Remember that they are all half naked since the ceremonial killing of the lice, except for the young man and the* MINISTER OF AGRICULTURE.

PRESIDENT: *Et tu* General? You have turned against me? Anyway I am not surprised. You don't think I know that you once planned a coup against me? Why did you think I made you a minister? To bring you closer so I could watch you and see to it that you're not up to any mischief. You see I was right about you? Ungrateful wretch! I made you feel important by making you implement my decrees. Treacherous son of a viper!

GENERAL: Wise One, you brought this upon yourself. We were supposed to be working closely together but you did not even give me a hint that you were involved in this kind of sordidness.

PRESIDENT: You kept secrets from me too, didn't you? You all kept secrets from me. Aha! What about the road, eh? What about the painted road? Did anyone tell me about that? I made a fool of myself in the presence of the Pope, and no one told me a damn thing.

AGRICULTURE: What are we going to do with him?

JUSTICE: How did he send messages to our torturers? He has never come into contact with them in all these years.

YOUNG MAN: It may have been through his thoughts.

PRESIDENT: Not just crude thoughts, fool. I am much more advanced than that. It was through my dreams. I conjured the torturers up in my dreams, and they featured in them. I interacted with them in my dreams, and gave them all the information they wanted. Of course when there were urgent messages I communicated with them through my thoughts, during my moments of introspection.

HEALTH: This man is nothing but a dump of toxic waste!

She spits at him.

PRESIDENT: You spit at me now. But I am your own creation.

All the others join in the spitting.

PRESIDENT: What you enjoy doing is building gods, putting them on a pedestal, worshipping them for a day, and then throwing stones at them and knocking them down. You have a very short attention span in the admiration of the gods that you create!

Lights fade to black as they repeatedly spit at him, mustering as much phlegm as possible, and splashing him all over with it.

The Bells
of
Amersfoort

commissioned by
De Nieuw Amsterdam Theatergroep

The Bells of Amersfoort, a joint production of De Nieuw Amsterdam Theatergroep and Sibikwa Community Theatre, will open after the publication of this book, at Theatre De Balie, Kleine Gartmanplantsoen 10, Amsterdam, Netherlands, on 29 March 2002, and will tour the Netherlands for two months. The cast will consist of five actors from De Nieuw Amsterdam: Suzanne Bakker, Reinier Bulder, Maikel August van Hetten, Marie-Christine Op den Kelder and Marvin Kolk and four actors from Sibikwa: Professor Mavuso, Sibulele Gcilitshana, Masupha Thabang and Zakes Zakhele Simango.

Music composed by Zakes Mda

The play directed by Aram Adriaanse.

Cast

TAMI WALAZA ... A black South African woman in her late thirties.

JOHAN VAN DER BIJL ... A white Afrikaner man, middle-aged, a church minister.

LUTHANDO VELA ... Tami's black South African fiancé.

KATJA ... A beautiful Dutch girl, works for the Dutch-South Africa Solidarity Movement.

CATHARINA ... Tami's neighbour, across the street, obsessed with cleaning windows.

HELEEN ... A black Dutch sex worker.

MARTIJN ... Tami's friend, a drummer.

FRITZ ... A painter, across the street.

MZAMO ... A black South African bishop.

The actors who play the above roles play other, mostly anonymous, characters too as the occasion demands (e.g. children, chorus, dancers and so on).

Scene One

The stage is divided into three distinct acting areas, located in any manner the director may deem fit. These areas may even be represented by different levels on the stage. One represents TAMI Walaza's present world. The second represents the world she has left behind, which is also the world to which she will return. The third represents the world she will never reach, the world she observes from her window. She vicariously participates in this world as well, although it unfolds across the street. The three worlds, of course, will not necessarily remain static. Sometimes they may collide or even merge and become one world. As lights rise on her world, TAMI is discovered standing next to a barstool – the only piece of furniture on this set. On the barstool is a bottle of red wine, an elegant wine glass and an ashtray. On the floor next to the barstool is a shimmering trombone. She pours herself some wine and has a sip. As lights rise on the second world she looks at it expectantly. Nothing happens. It is bare.

TAMI [*as if addressing the blank space*]: At home there were aunts and uncles. There were grandmothers and grandfathers. There were friends and neighbours. And, of course, there was Luthando.

LUTHANDO *materialises in the blank space of the second world.*

LUTHANDO: Dear Tami, since you left, the boys have come out thrice. Maybe four times. I have lost count. And the rains continue to cut deeper into the already wounded earth, taking with them bits of soil from the barren hills into the Telle River. From the Telle River into the Orange River. From the Orange River into the Atlantic Ocean. The rich soil of our scarred Qhoboshane Valley enriches distant oceans. What do oceans want with our soil when they already own a world of sand? But it is the coming out that I want to tell you about. The last coming out of the boys from the initiation school of the mountain, where the cutting of the foreskin transformed boys into men.

TAMI: There were fights and there was making up. A little hating and a little loving. But most importantly, there was laughter. We knew how to laugh, and we laughed. Even when we were in pain. Dear Luthando, here they have everything. They have freedom. And everything that goes with it. They have done away with the restrictions that societies often impose on themselves. Yet everyone wears a sad face. No one smiles.

LUTHANDO: The last coming out had a particular meaning to me, Tami, because your younger brother was one of the initiates. And he asked me specially to be there since you could not be there. I was there on your behalf, Tami, and everyone recognised that fact. They smiled at me and pampered me. They said, 'At least Luthando is here. He will eat the meat on Tami's behalf.' And I ate the meat on your behalf. And drank the beer on your behalf. [*Chuckles.*] Even though I know you don't drink.

TAMI *takes two guilty gulps from her wineglass.*

LUTHANDO: You always hated anything with alcohol in it. So, I ate on your behalf, but drank on my own behalf. Just a little sorghum beer. I wouldn't want to be drunk and disgrace myself in front of my future in-laws now, would I?

TAMI: Dear Luthando, when the sky clears a little and a few malnourished rays hit the gloomy faces of the people here, it is a miracle. Gloom melts away. Everybody looks to the heavens and says, 'The sun is up!'

LUTHANDO: But I did dance a little. Well, not just a little. I danced up a storm. You know I cannot resist it. Especially when the beer runs to my head.

He claps his hands and sings a song of the umtshotsho *ceremony. Slowly he begins to move his body in the* tyityimba *dance. A chorus enters and kneels in a half-moon around him, singing and drumming in accompaniment. At first* TAMI *looks at him in amazement. Then she claps for him as his dance gathers momentum. She cannot help but join in the dance. Although each of them is dancing in his or her own pool of light, in two different worlds, they are obviously dancing together. They*

115

keep the same rhythm and respond to one another. They are dancing the same dance. The dance becomes more frenzied and the drumming faster. They are out of breath but they continue to dance. Then his pool of light fades to black. In an instant he is no longer there. The chorus is no longer there either. She remains dancing alone, oblivious of the fact that he is no longer there and that no one is accompanying her stray song with drumming and handclapping. But soon enough she realises that she is dancing alone. She stops. She obviously feels foolish. She giggles, and then breaks into laughter. She is laughing at herself. She sheepishly goes back to her wine and takes a deep sip. She lights a cigarette, and inhales deeply.

TAMI [*sighs*]: After action! He was always like that, Luthando. Left me hanging. My body burning with desire to go on and on and on. He could never go the distance. Frenzied action then everything fizzles out and dies. Left me an unfulfilled woman. But we knew that our love for each other would overcome that little problem.

There is a knock. She does not respond. Instead she takes a sip from the glass. A knock again. KATJA enters. She is carrying a plastic bag full of a variety of fruit. TAMI does not turn to look at her.

KATJA: Maybe you should lock the door if you want to stop intruders like me.

TAMI: Maybe you people should give me a break.

KATJA: We are not the enemy, you know?

TAMI: I know ... I know ... I am my own enemy. I cannot help it if I am in this self-destructive mode.

KATJA: I have brought you some fruit.

She places the plastic bag on the floor next to the trombone.

TAMI: An offering of fruit for the goddess. From her faithful supplicants.

KATJA: Whatever happened to 'thank you'?

TAMI: What do you want me to say, Katja? Thanks, you didn't bring food this time?

KATJA: You don't like the food I bring? I can change the menu. Maybe you like cold food, no? Sandwiches ... cheese and ham? The best Gouda?

TAMI: I don't like you to bring me anything, Katja. No food, no fruit, nothing! I am a refugee, not an invalid. You people don't have to treat me like an invalid. You make me feel so useless. So dependent ... just sitting here ... doing nothing. Just getting fed. Like you are fattening me for slaughter.

KATJA [*hurt*]: You should have told me you didn't like the food. I wouldn't have bothered.

TAMI: So don't bother, missy, don't bother!

KATJA: The Dutch-South Africa Solidarity Movement sends me here to see to it that you are comfortable ... that your needs are met.

TAMI: The ugly food does not meet my needs.

KATJA: So you tell me now.

TAMI: The English are world famous for their terrible cooking. I think the world forgot about the Dutch. They match the English pound for pound.

KATJA [*laughs*]: That's being really ungracious to your hosts!

TAMI: I am not in the mood to be nice today, Katja.

KATJA: You are not in the mood to be nice any day.

TAMI: You wouldn't be in a nice mood either if you were cooped up in this musty flat all day long.

KATJA: And who is keeping you here? You are your own prisoner, Tami. You refuse to go out. You just want to sit here and stew in your self-pity. When you first came you were quite different. You used to be carefree.

TAMI: It was just a mask. Painted with a happy face.

KATJA: You used to honour invitations to talk about the situation back home. You used to attend demonstrations. You used to visit friends. What happened to you, Tami?

TAMI: I wouldn't be here burdening you with my problems if your people had not forced me out of my country?

KATJA: My people?

TAMI: The Boers ... the Afrikaners ... They came from here, didn't they?

KATJA: We cannot take all the credit for creating those people ... the Afrikaners. Some of their ancestors came from France. Go blame the French as well!

TAMI: Before the cock crows twice you have denied them!

KATJA: My people are the ones who have sent me to look after you. To see to it that you are comfortable. My people are the ones who are worrying that you seem to be sinking deeper into an alcoholic abyss.

TAMI: To salve their consciences?

KATJA: Go to hell!

TAMI [*chuckles*]: I am already there.

KATJA: And what's nice about it is that you have sent yourself there. With wine. How many bottles of wine do you drink a day?

TAMI *does not answer, but looks at her defiantly, and pours herself another glass.*

KATJA: I know ... you were looking for some medicine that you could drink and that would give you happiness.

TAMI: I was not looking for happiness. I just wanted to numb the pain.

KATJA: The pain?

TAMI: Of the bells.

KATJA: That is nonsense. You think you have discovered the remedy in these cheap bottles of wine. But you are wrong. Alcohol is no such medicine. Instead it will take you down the drain with it.

TAMI: Don't you dare preach to me. Did the comrades send you here to reform me? Did they? To preach to me? What would you know about it? What experience do you have of it? Damn nothing, I bet! You are just a spoilt little girl who grew up in the protective cocoon of a caring society. You wouldn't know a damn thing about hardship. You wouldn't know a bloody damn thing about the things that have happened to me.

KATJA: Of course I have no experience of the things that have happened to you. But I know that there are many other exiles here and in other countries who have gone through similar experiences. Yet they don't wallow in self-pity. They don't become wine-junkies. They participate actively in the life of the communities that have accepted them. They don't shun or despise the assistance of their hosts. They are actively working for the liberation of their country. Like you used to do when you first arrived.

TAMI: So, you think I can liberate my country from Holland?

KATJA: And, by the way, I am not some spoilt brat from some rich family who has so much time in her hands that she decides to do some charitable work for ungrateful refugees. Not everyone is well off in this country. I grew up on a houseboat on one of the canals of Amsterdam. Without a mother. She died quite early from alcohol abuse. I was brought up by an unemployed father who was also an alcoholic. I have seen the devastation that alcohol can cause to people ... to families.

TAMI: I am sorry. I did not know.

KATJA: Don't be sorry. I am not. I made something of my life. You can too.

TAMI: Oh, Katja, I am not strong enough not to be crushed by loneliness!

The bells toll. At first softly, and then in crescendo until they become very loud. TAMI freezes and the glass she is holding crashes to the floor. She is obviously in agony. At first KATJA does not know how to deal with the situation. Then she holds TAMI in her arms while TAMI writhes in pain. The bells stop and her agony ceases.

KATJA: I don't understand how such beautiful bells can have such a devastating effect on you.

TAMI [*laughing*]: I am so stupid, Katja! So very stupid!

Lights fade to black.

Scene Two

TAMI *enters the first world. She is carrying two wine bottles in a plastic bag. She walks unsteadily, obviously not completely sober. It is very cold and she is dressed accordingly. Lights rise on the second world and* LUTHANDO *enters. It is important that when the two lovers talk they are not looking at each other. They do not address each other directly since they are, in reality, thousands of kilometres apart. It must therefore be clear that they communicate with each other without seeing each other.*

LUTHANDO: Dear Tami, years have passed. The world you knew is no longer the same. It is changing every day. Even we who live in it can no longer recognise it. Cannot keep up with the changes. There are talks about talks. And then there are talks. We are now talking with the enemy, Tami. Freedom is coming. It is a different world. One thing hasn't changed though: floods continue to steal our soil into the rivers and into the seas. The land is left emaciated, with contours of ribs showing on its surface. Everyone has left for better places. No one has stayed to heal the land. I cannot hold on any longer, Tami. Many years have passed.

TAMI: You promised, Luthando, that you would wait for me ... that we'd heal the land together. You have been strong for so many years. You cannot give up now.

LUTHANDO: Dear Tami, exiles are coming back home in droves. Where are you? We do not see your face among the throngs that are arriving.

TAMI: I am coming ... I am coming. Let me battle with my demons first. Let me come home in victory. Not in shame.

LUTHANDO *shakes his head and prepares to go. For the first time* TAMI *turns and looks at him appealingly. She tries to reach for him.*

TAMI: You can't give up on me now, Luthando.

But he is too far away. He exits as darkness falls on his world.

TAMI [*frantically and drunkenly*]: Dear Luthando, did you receive the postcards that I sent you? Did you see how beautiful Amersfoort is? It is a quiet and serene place. Yet there is no quietness in me. Because of the demons that have got hold of me. They started first with loneliness, and then they grew into something unrecognisable. I do want to come back. I long to return like those who have returned. But I am shaking with fear. I must first extract myself from the hole that I dug myself into. I told you about Katja. The people here have been nice ... very nice. But still it is not home. I remain a foreigner. I can never be truly part of them. Dear Luthando, you will come back, won't you? [*Shouting angrily.*] You will come back, damnit! [*Then kindly and with softness.*] Dear Luthando, yesterday I was walking here at Onze Lieve Vrouwe Square, under the shadow of Long John ... I told you about Long John when I sent you the postcards ... the remnants of the cathedral from whose tower the bells that torture me come ... [*Laughs.*] I am tortured by the bells that come from the second highest tower in the Netherlands ... Yesterday I was walking under the shadow of Long John when I saw one swallow. One stray swallow doesn't make a spring, right? Then today I saw a whole flock of them. *Inkonjane.* The swallow. I knew exactly where they came from. That they have flown from your world. Some of them might even have seen you. Might even have built their mud nests under your eaves. It is April. Your autumn. Our spring. They have flown thousands of kilometres in just one month. Remember the song of the swallows that we used to sing? [*She sings*]:

> *Inkonjane emnyama*
> *Yabhabha emafini*
> *Walil'umntana*
> *Izembe lelam*

We sang the song of the swallows even though it never made any sense: the black swallow, flies in the sky, the child is crying, the axe is mine. What on earth was it all about? Dear Luthando, the swallows have come back before time, only to find that it is spring only in name. Snow still covers the ground. Here at the

Onze Lieve Vrouwe Square chairs and tables are stacked outside the cafés. Flurries of snow are still falling. No one will sit outside in this ugly weather. No one will venture out. Except those who must replenish their wine supplies [*brandishes the bottles she is carrying*]. And the children who throw snowballs at each other.

TAMI [*sings again*]:
> Inkonjane emnyama
> Yabhabha emafini, etc.

Enter two or three children chasing each other, miming gathering snow from the ground, shaping it into balls and throwing it at each other. Sometimes a child misses, sometimes he/she hits the target. All this is done with joyous shrieks and screams. They see TAMI singing and spinning around like a swallow in flight. They go to her and watch her curiously. She becomes aware of them and stops. She giggles in embarrassment. The children join her in laughter [Note that the children are played by the same adult actors who play the chorus.]

CHILD 1: What strange language was that?

They excitedly surround TAMI.

TAMI: It is called isiXhosa. It is spoken in South Africa.

The children try to click 'isiXhosa', with disastrous results. They find this very funny and laugh at their hopeless efforts.

TAMI: It is the song of the swallows.
CHILD 2: Teach us the song of the swallows.
TAMI: I'll teach you another isiXhosa song instead.

Immediately the children hear the click in 'isiXhosa' they try saying it and laugh.

TAMI [*sings*]:
> Ndiquqa le ezingqeleni
> Ndiqaqanjelwa yintliziyo
> Ndaqala ndiqumbhile ezingqeleni
> Ndiqhutywa zingqondo
> Zobubhanxa nobuxelegu

Ndaqala ndiqumbhile ezingqeleni
Ndagqibela ndiqalasa ndiqaqamba

The CHILDREN *join in the song. At first they struggle with the clicks,*
but soon enough they get the hang of it.

CHILD 3: What does it mean?
TAMI: It says I am out there in the cold, with a sore heart. I am sad
because I was sent here by my foolishness and carelessness. But
at the end of it all, my face will be bright and happy.
CHILD 1: It is a sad song.
CHILD 2: So how come it makes us dance?
TAMI: We dance to sad songs. [*She sings again*]
Ndiquqa le ezingqeleni
Ndiqaqanjelwa yintliziyo, etc. etc.

The CHILDREN *join and dance around her. They imitate her as she*
performs an isiXhosa dance. They all dance out in different directions,
waving goodbye to each other.

Lights fade to black.

Scene Three

Same as in Scene One. But Tami is not there. There is only a wine glass
on the barstool, without the bottle. The trombone still lies on the floor.
Enter KATJA.

KATJA: At least she keeps the room clean. Too sparkling clean if
you ask me. Clinically clean. Nothing lived in about this room.

She picks up the trombone and tries to blow it. She struggles. She can only
manage one rough note, which drains her, and she coughs. TAMI *enters,*
carrying her plastic bag of wine bottles. She is not amused.

TAMI: Nobody touches my instrument, do you hear me?
KATJA: Oh, come on, Tami. It's just a trombone. I am not going to
eat it.

TAMI: To you it is just a trombone. To me it is more than that.

KATJA: Still use it to attract the anger of the neighbours?

TAMI: It is the only way to get them to talk to me. When they shout and bang at the walls and scream that I am making a noise. I don't know why noise scares them so much. Noise is the essence of life. I can't help it that you Dutch people can't handle chaos. It destabilises you completely.

KATJA: You went to buy more wine.

TAMI: A very clever observation. Indeed these are two bottles of wine. What have you brought me this time?

KATJA: Nothing.

TAMI: Nothing? How can you not bring me anything? Damnit man, you always bring me something.

KATJA: Until you complained that I am making you an invalid.

TAMI: Since when do you listen to my complaints? [*Moaning.*] This is very cruel. You make me get used to your bringing me something to eat, and then all of a sudden you stop. First you make me feel dependent and useless and pitiful. And then all of a sudden I must strive on my own. This is very unreasonable.

KATJA [*jokingly*]: Now you know what I am capable of when I am pushed too far.

TAMI: You should have told me before hand, man. Then I would have made other arrangements. I would have bought stuff. You made me an invalid, now you expect me to stand up and run!

KATJA: Ja-ja, stand up and run.

TAMI *defiantly turns her back on* KATJA, *opens a bottle of wine and pours herself a drink.*

KATJA: To me that doesn't look like the best way of standing up and running.

TAMI: So what do you want here if you haven't brought me anything?

KATJA: To see that you are all right ... you are comfortable.

TAMI: I am all right, then go.

KATJA: We are in a foul mood today, aren't we?

TAMI: It's not my fault that you bring out the worst in me. In one sentence – 'I haven't brought you anything to eat' – you have erased the little sunshine that the children brought in my life.

KATJA: The children? Whose children?

TAMI: At the Onze Lieve Vrouwe Square. We sang and danced.

KATJA [*incredulously*]: You sang and danced? With the children? In the street?

TAMI: Why does that surprise you?

KATJA: You who sit here all day long moping and drowning yourself in wine? There is hope yet!

TAMI: Don't you start with me again, Katja. You are such a nag!

KATJA: Don't you want to know where I was this morning?

TAMI: No.

KATJA: I'll tell you all the same. I was at Schipol Airport. Bidding farewell to some of your comrades. They are going back home.

TAMI: Good luck to them.

KATJA: And you?

TAMI: What about me?

KATJA: You haven't thought of ...?

TAMI: Going back to South Africa? Are you tired of me now? Want to get rid of me at your earliest convenience? I knew sooner or later it would come to this.

KATJA [*laughs*]: You know that I wouldn't mind if you stayed here forever.

TAMI: Don't lie.

KATJA: This has become your home. You have lived with us here for years. But I am sure South Africa does need you too, Tami. Your skills. The skills that you have never used since you graduated from college. A degree in rural development, and it is just wasted while you sit here and pickle yourself in alcohol.

TAMI *does not respond. There is a pause while she gulps her wine and* KATJA *looks out of a presumed window.*

KATJA: Your neighbour across the street ... the woman ... I haven't seen her do anything but clean the window.

Lights rise on the third world. We see CATHARINA *briskly cleaning the window and humming a song.* TAMI *joins* KATJA *at the window.*

TAMI: That is Catharina. She likes to clean her window. She cleans it all day long.

KATJA: Oh, so you know her name? You have spoken with her?

TAMI: No, I don't know her. I just gave her that name. She looks like a Catharina to me so she is Catharina.

KATJA: And in the window below Catharina's?

Lights fall on CATHARINA *and rise on* FRITZ, *on the same third world. The song* CATHARINA *was humming continues.* FRITZ *has a canvas on an easel and is furiously painting a bright picture. He is humming his own Dutch song, which combines well with Catharina's song.*

TAMI: He paints all day long. I haven't named him yet. I can't think of an appropriate name.

KATJA: He is Fritz. He looks like a Fritz to me.

TAMI: Ja, Fritz, that's a good name for him.

KATJA: And in the next window? There is no one there. Just a well-made bed covered with a grey duvet with yellow flowers.

TAMI: You shouldn't be looking at that window.

KATJA: Why?

TAMI: Because it is Monday. At midday you will see things you are not supposed to see.

Lights fall on FRITZ *and rise on* JOHAN VAN DER BIJL. *He is dressed in a dark suit and dog-collar. He walks solemnly, reading the Bible to himself.*

KATJA: Have you given that one a name too?

TAMI: I just call him Dominee. He is a good man throughout the week, except at midday on Mondays and Fridays. Then he becomes very very naughty. Mondays are red days. Fridays are black days.

KATJA: What happens on Mondays and Fridays?

TAMI: You will see. Don't be in a hurry. At midday you'll see.

KATJA: See what, Tami? Don't do this to me!

TAMI: Heleen ... I have named her too ... Heleen will come at midday and fuck his brains out. No ceremony. No foreplay. No communication. She just comes and ...

KATJA: Is that how you spend your time on Mondays and Fridays? Being a voyeur? Why haven't I seen this before?

TAMI: Because you usually come on Tuesdays and Saturdays. Except today. I don't know why you came today. Oh, yeah. To gloat that you have come from seeing some people off at the airport. To give me the loud hint that it's high time I packed my bags and left.

At this moment HELEEN *enters the third world. She is wearing a red coat and red pencil-heel shoes. She does not acknowledge the dominee. To the rhythm of Catharina's and Fritz's song she takes off her coat. She is not wearing a dress. She remains only in her red panties, red bra and red stockings with a red garter. She spreads her arms to say 'I am ready for you'. The dominee, also to the rhythm, takes off his pants and his jacket. He remains in his black shirt and dog-collar. He spreads his arms to say 'Me too'. They make furious love. But note that this lovemaking is highly stylised. They do it standing and must not even touch each other. There must be a distance between them. Catharina's voice rises to the level of a high-pitched aria, while Fritz's voice becomes deep humming. None of the grunts associated with sexual pleasure. Joyous humming, backing Catharina's wayward song. Lights fall on the love makers and rise on* CATHARINA *cleaning the window and singing. Then they fall on her and rise on* FRITZ *painting and singing. This is repeated a few times, the lights rising and falling in a confused manner. This rising and falling and the high-pitched aria stun* KATJA *while they excite* TAMI. *She takes her trombone and blows up a storm. She blows and blows and blows .... until the aria and the lovemaking reach a climax. And then everything stops. Lights have fallen on the third world.* TAMI *sighs in fulfilment, as if she herself has been making love. She lovingly holds her trombone close to her chest.* KATJA *reverses out, until she exits.* TAMI *lights a cigarette and spreads herself on the floor to relax.* KATJA *comes running back.*

KATJA: You know, Tami, I have been thinking ...

TAMI: That makes a change, doesn't it?

KATJA: You can make yourself useful by teaching those children at the square Xhosa dances. You know ... some drumming and some dancing. That would keep you busy and earn you a few extra gilders.

TAMI: Who says they want to learn isiXhosa dances? What will they do with the dance of the amaXhosa?

KATJA: You know, kids are always interested to learn more about Africa. And their parents will pay in the name of the new ethos of multi-culturalism. A little drumming and a little foot-stomping.

TAMI: I know nothing about drumming.

KATJA: What kind of a black person are you who knows nothing about drumming? Never mind. I have a friend who plays the drums. Martijn. He is black too. From Surinam. Stays in Amsterdam though. I am sure Martijn would be happy to drum for you while you tell stories and dance. You can even play your trombone if you like. Not only will you teach the children, you can even have gigs.

TAMI: Don't get carried away, Katja.

KATJA: You can have gigs. Black people are storytellers, aren't they? You can have storytelling and dancing gigs. You and your trombone. Martijn and his drums. Maybe add a guitar somewhere there.

TAMI: You make it sound so attractive. I am not really a performer, but here ... who will know the difference? Bring that bloody Martijn here!

KATJA: Once I get him you'll be the first to know.

She exits in excitement. TAMI *remains puffing on her cigarette and sipping her wine nonchalantly. The bells toll. She winces in pain.*

TAMI: You know, this is a lovely town, if only they could stop the goddamned bells!

Lights fade to black.

Scene Four

Lights rise simultaneously on the first and second worlds. TAMI *and* LUTHANDO *are discovered in the middle of their correspondence.*

LUHANDO: We are free, Tami, we are free. After almost four hundred years we are free. The burden of humiliation has been removed from our shoulders. We are now able to walk straight; our bodies are no longer bent forwards. We are no longer crouching. We walk straight and tall and our bodies are strong, fed with the milk of freedom. Is that not what you and I fought for, Tami? Now we have got it. Come back, Tami. Come back.

TAMI: Dear Luthando, it has been many months since I heard from you. Seasons of swallows have come and gone. Hope has blossomed and wilted. The demons continue to eat my insides. I am a seeker, Luthando. I have always been a seeker. Perhaps that is why I am here. I am a seeker, but I do not know what I seek.

LUTHANDO: How will you know when you find it?

TAMI: When I find it I will not seek anymore. And the demons that are eating me shall disappear from my life. But your silence will kill me long before then.

LUTHANDO: It is difficult, Tami. I am sorry I have been silent. But things have not been easy. While you are battling with what you refer to as your demons ... the demons I don't understand ... we here have been having our own battles. It is not easy to be free after nearly four hundred years. We do not know how to deal with this freedom yet. We still need to be taught how to be free. You should be here, Tami. We should be fumbling together. We should be discovering together how to be free.

TAMI: I am coming, Luthando. Give me time. I have kept my promises to you. I have kept myself for you.

LUTHANDO: I do not believe you have kept the promises. We promised each other that we would heal the wounded earth. Even though we eat the fruits of freedom, the earth is not healed yet. The damage is too deep to be healed by a stroke of the pen.

We need to work with our hands, Tami, as we promised ourselves and our people. We need to heal the land with the warmth of our hands.

TAMI: Let me heal myself first.

LUTHANDO: How did they begin, these demons that possess you? Where do they come from?

TAMI: It all started with loneliness. A searing loneliness. A longing for the world I had left behind. And the bells. The bells toll every day. At first I drank to numb the pain of the bells. And in no time I was deep in the bottle, Luthando. I, who hated anything with alcohol in it, was deep in the bottle. Now I am afraid. I cannot face my people drenched in wine like this. Me, their daughter who was so full of promise. I know the glowing reports that the whole of Qhoboshane Valley received, of how I excelled at university in Holland, passing with flying colours a degree in development studies and economics. Let me heal myself first, Luthando.

LUTHANDO: I will stand by you, Tami. I will stand by you because I know of the things that have happened to you, that broke you and drove you into all this. It was your strength and your love for our people. I know how the road you took started. I was part of that road.

TAMI: Yes, Luthando. It all started with the bells.

LUTHANDO: Perhaps we should start from the beginning. The very beginning. It all started with a wedding.

TAMI [*smiles fondly at the memory*]: Oh, yes, the wedding!

LUTHANDO: We had not made our vows yet. The minister had not yet declared us man and wife.

TAMI: That means nothing to me. What is important is that we were there in church. In the process of making the vows.

MZAMO *enters in the second world. He is dressed in the maroon of a bishop.* LUTHANDO *and* TAMI *exit.*

MZAMO: Dearly beloved, we are gathered here today to bond the two lovers, Tami Walaza and Luthando Vela, with the super-glue of holy matrimony.

Soon the wedding SINGERS *and* DANCERS *join* MZAMO *as he chants and dances. They sing, dance and ululate.*

Enter TAMI *and* LUTHANDO. *They are the bride and the bridegroom. The* SINGERS *dance around them. The couple fall into step with them. The singing and drumming rise to a frenzied pitch, and then on a cue from* MZAMO *everything freezes.* LUTHANDO *and* TAMI *hold each other's hands as they begin to take the vows.*

LUTHANDO: To love and to honour.
TAMI: To love and to cherish.

The SINGERS *hum the wedding song softly.*

TAMI: To heal the wounded earth.
LUTHANDO: Yes, to heal the scarred earth.

The DRUMMER *begins to drum and* LUTHANDO *breaks into a frenzied dance, dancing for his bride. The* DANCERS *ululate.* MZAMO *chants. All of a sudden sirens are wailing. Blue police lights are flashing. There is panic among the wedding singers. They all run in different directions in a confused manner. The bride and groom just stand there stunned. A* POLICE OFFICER *enters. Even in the confusion of the blue flashing lights we can clearly identify him as* JOHAN VAN DER BIJL.

LUTHANDO: You can't do this. Not at our wedding.
JOHAN: You will not obstruct the law if you know what is good for you. It is she we want, not you.

JOHAN *is putting handcuffs on* TAMI.

LUTHANDO: But we had not finished taking the vows. Can't we just finish the ceremony? Guests have come from faraway places. They want to see a complete wedding. What has she done? What do you want with her? You can't do this Captain Johan van der Bijl.

JOHAN *leads* TAMI *out.* LUTHANDO *remains on the stage stunned. Lights fade to dark.*

Scene Five

Tami's world. She is not there. Only her trombone and an empty glass.
KATJA and MARTIJN enter. He is carrying a drum.

MARTIJN: I see she takes her music seriously.

KATJA: Not really. She takes her wine seriously. She only uses the trombone to annoy the neighbours.

MARTIJN takes the trombone and tries to blow it.

KATJA: Don't touch that. She gets annoyed when anybody touches her instrument.

But MARTIJN *continues to blow discordant notes.*

MARTIJN: An odd choice of instrument. You don't find many women playing the trombone.

KATJA: She took it up when she came here. Self-taught. She's still not that good at it, although she thinks she is.

MARTIJN: Drumming and trombone. That is a ridiculous combination, isn't it?

KATJA: Drumming and storytelling, that's what I had in mind. And maybe singing African songs. Of course, she may insist on playing the trombone. I am sure you'll find a way around that.

MARTIJN: Can she sing then?

KATJA: I thought every black person could sing.

MARTIJN: Just like every black person can dance? Katja, I thought you brought me here for something serious. Something meaningful.

KATJA: It may turn out to be more meaningful than you think. She is beautiful.

MARTIJN: Are you saying what I think you are saying?

KATJA: She often says she is a seeker. Has been looking for something since childhood. But never really knew what it was. Her loneliness is the loneliness of a seeker. I think she looked in the wrong places. Maybe you are *it*.

MARTIJN: It?

KATJA: The thing she has been looking for.

MARTIJN [*laughs*]: Does she know you are trying to be a matchmaker?

KATJA: Not quite. She thinks my interests lie only in setting up a small band that will keep her busy and take her mind off the wine.

MARTIJN: What makes you think I'd want to go out with an alcoholic?

KATJA [*adamantly*]: She is not an alcoholic. She is just lonely, that's all. And thinks that wine will give her happiness. She needs a beautiful strong man like you. She is an intelligent woman. Someone you could be serious about.

MARTIJN: Serious? So you have you already set the wedding date?

KATJA: A woman with great values.

MARTIJN [*mockingly*]: A woman from Mother Africa!

He beats his drum and chants some gibberish that has the sounds of some African language. He mockingly dances around KATJA, which annoys her no end.

KATJA: Don't be silly, Martijn!

But MARTIJN is bent on ridiculing her, so he continues with his silly dance. At this stage TAMI enters with her two bottles of wine. MARTIJN stops.

TAMI: Don't mind me. Go on with your concert in my flat.

MARTIJN [*embarrassed*]: I am sorry.

KATJA: This is Martijn, Tami.

TAMI: Is he a substitute for the food you used to bring me?

MARTIJN: I can be that if you want me to be.

KATJA: He is the drummer I told you about.

TAMI: The drummer you told me about? What drummer?

KATJA: The one who is going to drum for you when you sing and tell stories and do your African dances.

TAMI: Who says I'll be doing all those things?

KATJA: But you agreed. You said I could bring the drummer.

TAMI: I said no such thing. Now if you will excuse me.

MARTIJN: You know, I came all the way from Amsterdam because I heard you are a nice African lady who wants to share her beautiful culture with the rest of Holland. But it seems I was wrong.

TAMI: Who ever told you that made a fool of you.

MARTIJN: You know, we could make a beautiful team. People from Surinam and from South Africa are here to enrich Holland ... to give it a multicultural tint that it did not have. You can enrich it with your stories and your songs and your dances.

TAMI *takes a close look at him as if she is inspecting an ox for sale.*

TAMI: Mhh ... Big voice and broad gestures.

MARTIJN *teasingly flexes his muscles.*

MARTIJN: Well, I am a black man, am I not? Look at black people wherever they are ... they have a manner of walking that is expansive. That is big and broad. As if they are not slaves. As if they own the place.

TAMI *cannot help but laugh. The others join in her laughter. Lights fade to black.*

Scene Six

Lights rise on TAMI. *She is taking a casual stroll.*

TAMI: Dear Luthando, it is a hot summer.

Lights rise on LUTHANDO. *He is driving a well-made wire car, the kind that township kids create as toys. It is an accurate representation of a BMW.*

LUTHANDO: Dear Tami. It is a cold winter.

TAMI: I have been walking around the town. I walked for kilometres without going anywhere in particular. Just walked. In circles even. And every time I return to the shadow of the Onze Lieve Vrouwe tower.

LUTHANDO: Fortunately my car is air-conditioned. Did I tell you I bought a new car? A BMW Three-Series? I am driving around, thinking warm thoughts about you.

TAMI: Often I pretend to be lost so that I may ask for directions. Today I got lost for real. Lost inside myself. It is a heavy vow that we made to each other, Luthando. That we would keep each other for each other. Come what may. I have won, Luthando. I have kept myself for you, even though my life is not devoid of temptations.

LUTHANDO: Dear Tami, those vows ... don't you think we were young and foolish? Yes, we were young and foolish and overzealous. We made promises that were beyond us. Oceans and seasons separate us. We are human. I for one have to satisfy the needs of the flesh. I am a man.

TAMI: I satisfy them at my window. On Mondays and Fridays. I can tell you about this because we have always been open with each other. On Mondays and Fridays my trombone finds work, and I get the fulfilment. It works well for all of us. My body remains pure and untouched, waiting just for you. Yet my needs are fulfilled.

LUTHANDO: You have found a way, I have not.

TAMI: What are you trying to tell me, Luthando? That you have not been faithful to me?

LUTHANDO: I am saying that it is more difficult for a man.

TAMI: Answer me, damnit!

LUTHANDO: Don't blame me, Tami. Don't blame me.

TAMI: Oh, my God! How could you?

LUTHANDO: You have your demons I have mine. We got free, Tami, and I became a highflier. I cannot help it, Tami. It is the fault of freedom. I didn't know I had this fetish ... to make love to powerful women. And there are many of them since we got liberated. Leaders in their fields. In Parliament. In the Cabinet nogal. In the corporate world. What is a man with a fetish expected to do? Wait for a wife ... no, a fiancée, for we had not completed our wedding vows when Johan van der Bijl broke up our wedding ... wait for a fiancée who is refusing to come home even long after we have gained our liberation? You could have been one of the powerful women too, Tami. With your university degree and my political party connections you would have been very powerful. And my fetish would have been satisfied.

He exits, leaving TAMI *astounded. Enter The* REV. JOHAN VAN DER BIJL *in the first world. He is engrossed in reading the Bible.*

JOHAN [*reading*]: ' ... When the Lord therefore of the vineyard cometh, what will he do unto those husbandmen? They say unto him, He will miserably destroy those wicked men, and will let out *his* vineyard unto other husbandmen, which shall render him the fruits in their seasons. Jesus saith unto them, Did ye never read in the scriptures, The stone which the builders rejected, the same is become the head of the corner: this is the Lord's doing, and it is marvellous in our eyes? Therefore say I unto you, The kingdom of God shall be taken from you, and given to a nation bringing forth the fruits thereof' [Matthew 21:40-43].

TAMI: Can you believe the cheek of this man? I kept myself for him for so many years. Almost died of loneliness. And today he confesses that he has been fucking every powerful woman in South Africa.

JOHAN: God bless you, my child.

Recognition dawns on TAMI's *face.*

TAMI: Hey, I know you.

JOHAN: Have we been introduced?

TAMI: You are the Dominee.

JOHAN: Of course, I am a dominee. Any moron can see that.

TAMI: Not just a dominee. *The* Dominee.

JOHAN *is puzzled.*

TAMI: Very very naughty on Mondays and Fridays.

JOHAN [*taken aback*]: Has she been talking about me?

TAMI: Heleen never talks. I have never even met her.

JOHAN: Heleen?

TAMI: The woman who fucks your brains out every Monday and Friday. I have named her Heleen.

JOHAN: Heleen? You have been spying on me, haven't you?

TAMI: I never spy, Dominee. I have better things to do than spy on you. I look out of my window and there you are, flaunting yourself for all the world to see!

JOHAN: The curtains! I never thought somebody could be watching.

TAMI: Who is she, Dominee?

JOHAN: She is Heleen. You said so yourself.

TAMI: I know she's Heleen, but who the hell is she.

JOHAN: *Dit is nie die tipe taal wat 'n goeie Godvresende vrou behoort te gebruik nie.*

(That's not the kind of language a good, God-fearing woman should be using.)

TAMI: Hey, that's not Dutch! That's Afrikaans! Who the hell are you?

JOHAN: How do you know it's Afrikaans? Ah, I see, you are from South Africa!

TAMI *finds* JOHAN's *discomfort amusing.*

TAMI: You came all the way from South Africa to mess around with a mistress. A black one at that. Heleen can't be your wife. A wholesome boereseun like you cannot have a black wife.

JOHAN: And how would you know?

TAMI: I wonder if your congregation is aware of your secret life?

JOHAN: I have no congregation. At least not here. Back home, yes, I have a big congregation. I am here as a higher degree student at a theology college.

TAMI: Your wife ... does she know this is what you are up to in Holland?

JOHAN: I have always been faithful to my wife.

TAMI: Just like I have been faithful to my man, only to learn that he has been driving around in a BMW fucking himself to death.

JOHAN: I am a man of the cloth. I respect the sanctity of marriage. No one can accuse me of infidelity because there has never been any emotional involvement between Heleen and me. No attachment. Just the gratification of the flesh. It is written in the Holy Book that man shall not live by bread alone.

TAMI: Does Heleen know that she means so little to you?

JOHAN: Of course she does. I mean nothing to her either. It is a job. She is a sex worker.

TAMI: Ah, a prostitute. I should have guessed.

JOHAN: I first spotted her in a display window in the red light district of Amsterdam. There were women of different hues and shapes. Blondes, brunettes and redheads. Orientals and occidentals. But immediately I got to Heleen's window, I knew I should have her. I was struck by her golden brown legs. Black body parts. Forbidden fruit where I came from. I wanted her for myself. Not in her little sex cubicle but on my own turf. I negotiated and bargained until she agreed to come here twice a week. Of course, it costs me more for her to come all the way to Amersfoort. But it is worth it, I am sure you can bear witness to that.

TAMI: Don't mix me up in your sordid affairs.

JOHAN: Oh, you are mixed up in them all right. You have watched us. You have taken pains to watch us twice a week. Whether you like it or not you are a participant in my sordid affairs. You thought you were watching me, you did not know that an eye is always there ... looking at you, even when there is no one there. A much more powerful eye than yours.

TAMI: What nonsense are you trying to talk now?

JOHAN: Let me know when your next birthday is. I'll buy you a pair of binoculars so that you may have close-ups. Goodbye, young lady. And happy spying.

JOHAN *exits.* TAMI *follows him.*

TAMI [*indignantly*]: Hey, I was not spying on you. Wait, Dominee, you didn't tell me who you are. You look like somebody I know. Not from the window, no. From somewhere else. I have seen this man before! Dominee, wait!

She exits. Lights fade to black.

Scene Seven

TAMI *and* MARTIJN *are sitting on the floor facing each other. He is beating on a small drum between his legs.* CATHARINA *on the third world is cleaning the window and* FRITZ *is painting sunflowers. Their movements are consistent and monotonous so the focus will not be on them, but on* MARTIJN *and* TAMI. *This is helped by the fact that the lights are brighter on* TAMI *and* MARTIJN *than on the other pair.* MARTIJN *stops drumming to roll a cigarette.*

TAMI: You and your dagga!

MARTIJN: What is dagga?

TAMI: Grass, weed, pot, Mary-Jane ... whatever you choose to call it.

MARTIJN: The holy herb? Why should it bother you?

TAMI: In South Africa they would have locked you up long ago.

MARTIJN: Well, here it is legal. You can buy it at any coffee shop that displays a green light.

TAMI: I know ... I know ... A society without restrictions. Savouring the freedom of green and red lights! Life is like a traffic light. Red! Screw! Green! Smoke! Stop! Go! And now, of course, if you decide to die, you can die too ... without anyone taking issue with you.

MARTIJN *is puffing on his cigarette. Then he mockingly charges towards her, screaming like a madman, beating on the drum.*

MARTIJN: Come on, African woman, show me what you are made of!

TAMI: Okay, you asked for it. Don't complain.

She picks up her trombone and blows up a storm. The people in the third world brandish their fists in anger. It is like a silent movie; we can't hear what they say. We can only see their angry gestures, which become part of MARTIJN *and* TAMI's *mad dance. After the din has reached its peak the drumming and the trombone stop. Only the anger remains in the faces of the people of the third world as they continue their disturbed work of painting and cleaning the window.*

MARTIJN *and* TAMI *fall into each other's arms, laughing.*

MARTIJN: That was very wicked. You are lucky they haven't complained to the police about your wild noise.

TAMI: It is your fault. You bring out the wild tribal woman in me! Or perhaps the crazy township woman. I like it so much when Dutch people are destabilised by noise. There is too much order here. We need a little bit of chaos. Noise is normal where I come from. Loudspeakers blaring. Different types of music competing from neighbouring houses! Street noises. Children screaming. Dogs barking.

MARTIJN: And, of course, your trombone.

TAMI: No, I didn't play it when I was over there. I learnt it a few months after I had got here. Somehow it connected me to Luthando. He used to play the trombone in the Boy Scout band. That's how we met. I was in the drum majorettes and he played in the band.

MARTIJN: You still think of him? You still miss him?

TAMI: He has decided not to respond to my letters. He can go to hell. When I get back there he'll have a few questions to answer.

MARTIJN: I think you should forget about going back. You belong here now. We could make it big here. Very big!

TAMI: You belong here, Martijn. I don't. I must admit Holland has been very good to me. The people have been good. Katja. You. The folks at the Dutch-South Africa Solidarity Movement. This society is actively fighting against racism. On a chosen date and hour throughout the country bells ring to mark the day of anti-racism ... when people re-commit themselves to fight racism. I haven't seen anything like that anywhere else in Europe.

MARTIJN: Hey, have you recently been appointed the public relations officer or even chief propagandist of the Dutch establishment? The Dutch people have their apartheid too. It may be subtle. You may not see it. But it is still there. You will not see it when things are fine. But during the times when young people are unable to get jobs you'll certainly see it. The first people they'll blame are the foreigners. *Buiterlanders uit!* (Foreigners out!)

TAMI: Of course there may be instances of racism, especially from some individuals. But what is important is that there are efforts to fight it. There are good anti-racist structures. There is activism towards multi-culturalism. I love the openness of the Dutch society.

MARTIJN: Ah, and all these are your reasons for not staying?

TAMI: What I am telling you is that in spite of all the good things here, the longer I stay the more I feel I cannot be at home except in my own country. I have a longing for familiar things.

MARTIJN: For Luthando.

TAMI: No ... not for him ... for ordinary things ... the smells ... the rain ... the thunder.

MARTIJN: It rains here too.

TAMI: A different kind of rain. The gentle kind. I long for the rain that rains in big drops.

MARTIJN: Your rains are different. And your winters are cold. It snows.

TAMI: Some winters; some parts of the country.

MARTIJN: It is the only cold country I know where black people have their origins. How did they keep warm before the white man came?

TAMI: Do you seriously think warmth came with white people? Perhaps you must question the kind of history you were taught in Surinam ... or even here in Holland.

He returns to beating the drum.

MARTIJN: Come on, we don't have all day to rehearse. We can't just sit here talking. I have to catch the late afternoon train back to Amsterdam. [*With a naughty smirk.*] Unless of course you have designs on me.

TAMI: Did they also remember to teach you that we lived in trees before the white man came?

MARTIJN: Are we going to rehearse or not?

He beats the drum even more furiously. But she does not dance. She walks to the window and looks at FRITZ and CATHARINA still at their work. Then the lights rise on JOHAN VAN DER BIJL. HELEEN enters. She wears a black coat.

TAMI: It is Heleen's black day today.

MARTIJN *joins her at the window, still beating the drum. But he stops when he sees* HELEEN *stripping to her black underwear.* JOHAN *looks at* TAMI *and* MARTIJN. *He waves at them and closes the curtains. Darkness falls on* JOHAN *and* HELEEN. CATHARINA *sings her aria and* FRITZ *backs her.* MARTIJN *and* TAMI *hold each other and remain like statues. Lights fade to black.*

Scene Eight

Enter TAMI.

TAMI: Dear Luthando, Martijn heard Catharina and Fritz for the first time yesterday. He suggests that we should recruit them into our band. He thinks it will make ours a unique multi-cultural band: a woman who backs moans and groans of ecstasy with arias; a humming painter who paints sunflowers in the middle of a snow-covered winter; a Surinamese drummer in search of the Africa that history has buried somewhere deep inside him; and me, the African woman who continues to be a seeker. I am still alone, Luthando, even though I am surrounded by people. I am still a seeker. I am still alone.

Enter JOHAN VAN DER BIJL *from a different direction. He is not pleased to see her, although she is excited to see him.*

JOHAN: You again!

TAMI: Our paths are destined to cross, Dominee. It was quite a show yesterday. But did you have to close the curtains?

JOHAN: Next time I'll open them. I'll do it especially for you. Why, I'll even do it on the street for you. Or even in your living room.

TAMI: You don't have to go to that extreme. Just open the damned curtains, that's all. The way you used to do. That's not asking for too much.

JOHAN: Go get your own! The days of your pirating a ride on my horse are over. Finish and *klaar*.

TAMI: Admit it, Dominee, you like the idea that I am there. That is why you even waved at me. I wouldn't put it past you that somewhere in your imagination you have placed yourself between Heleen and me.

JOHAN: Don't flatter yourself.

TAMI: I need your help.

JOHAN: Sorry, I already have Heleen.

TAMI: Don't flatter *yourself*. I only need you to talk with your neighbours: the painter and the window cleaner. Catharina and Fritz. I want to recruit them for my band.

JOHAN: I don't know them. Never even seen them.

TAMI: But you have heard them. They sing for you every Monday and Friday.

JOHAN: I have heard them, yes, just like I have heard you with your atrocious trombone. And now you have that black man with the drums.

TAMI: We'll combine well, don't you think? All of us together. We would make a very good band. Maybe you and Heleen too. Why not?

JOHAN *laughs. She laughs too.*

JOHAN: I'd rather recruit Catharina and Fritz for you. Okay?

TAMI: You are a good man, Reverend.

There is a pause, while they contemplate each other.

JOHAN: I heard you, you know? You are a seeker. You are alone.

TAMI: It was supposed to be private correspondence with my man back home.

JOHAN: I can understand that. Loneliness, I mean. I am alone too. One becomes very alone in this country.

TAMI: You too? I would not have imagined it of you.

JOHAN: Because I am white?

TAMI: Not because you are white. Martijn is not white, yet he is part and parcel of this society.

JOHAN: Martijn?

TAMI: My drummer. It has nothing to do with being white. I would have thought you wouldn't have any difficulty integrating yourself into this society. After all, you are a Dutchman.

JOHAN: I'm an Afrikaner, not a Dutchman. It is an insult to call an Afrikaner a Dutchman.

TAMI: Your ancestors came from here, didn't they?

JOHAN: Of course they came from here. But the Afrikaner hasn't got an immediate memory of his Dutchness. The Afrikaner is an African and the Dutch are Europeans. The last political connection between the Afrikaner and the Dutch was during the Anglo-Boer War when the Dutch supported the Boers. Since then it has only been a spiritual connection, maintained by the church. That is why I am here for my higher education – following many NGK ministers over the years who have received their education here.

TAMI: I did not know that. I thought you would feel at home here.

JOHAN: I cannot say living in Holland has been difficult ... no ... but I never really settled in. I think of South Africa as home. I am a migrant. A *buiterlander*. Even though I speak the language. Even though I look like any Dutch person. I live for the day when I go back home.

TAMI: I thought it was only me. That there was something wrong with me. I am so glad that I have met you.

JOHAN: I, on the other hand, thought it would be easier for *you*. The people here are aligned with your struggle. And rejoice with you in your victory.

TAMI: Yes, I do meet people who are aligned with our political struggle, but we don't really become friends. We become political colleagues. Comrades in the struggle. But not friends.

JOHAN: They say it is my ancestral home, yet I come as a stranger. Don't think I have not tried to find a connection. To establish my roots, so to say. I have even gone to a village that bears my name. It is far removed from who I am. From what I am. I am of Africa. I do not feel part of this land. Even the soil smells differently.

TAMI [*emphatically*]: The smell of the soil. The peculiar smell of a gravel path after the rain.

JOHAN: How do you take that with you to Holland? How do you create that in Holland?

The bells begin to toll. TAMI *winces, but* JOHAN *does not notice.*

JOHAN: Here we stand at the centre ... the very centre ... of the land of Jan van Riebeeck. More than three hundred years of history separate us. Yet this is the centre. Do you know that? On this very spot near the tower, it is the centre of Holland? Under the shadow of Long John ...

As the bells continue to toll TAMI *is in agony.* JOHAN *runs to her assistance. It is as if each toll hits her in the stomach.* JOHAN *holds her until the bells stop.*

TAMI: I hate those bells.

JOHAN: Such beautiful bells! How can they have such an effect on you? Who are you? What is your story?

TAMI [*tiredly*]: They are very painful, these bells.

JOHAN: Every time they toll, they take me back to my home town in the Eastern Cape.

TAMI: In the Eastern Cape? They take me back there too.

JOHAN: On Sundays in Aliwal North the bells gathered the Lord's flock into his temple. And when the Orange River was flowing full, they reverberated from its waters. The bells of my youth. Their music rings in my ears to this day. It was an idyllic life. The whole rhythm of life was in those bells. Of course, things have changed. That idyllic life in towns like Aliwal North is gone. Liberation came. Blacks moved in. Whites moved out.

TAMI: Yes, in Aliwal North. That is where it all started. The bells reverberating. I knew I had met you somewhere before! You are Johan van der Bilj, are you not?

JOHAN: Of course, I am Johan van der Bijl. And you?

TAMI: I am the woman you arrested on her wedding day.

JOHAN [*discomfiture creeps in*]: Tami Walaza.

TAMI: You bastard, I am here because of you!

JOHAN: I am here because of you too.

TAMI: You bastard! You destroyed my life! You bloody well destroyed my life!

She exits in anger.

JOHAN: Hey, come back! We must talk about this! Tami Walaza

He also exits. Light fades on the first world. For sometime there is darkness on all three worlds. The bells toll again. But they seem to be quite distant now. Lights rise on the second world. TAMI is flung into the second world. She is wearing her wedding dress. But now it is soiled, torn and tattered. She sits there for a while as if stunned. JOHAN VAN DER BIJL, now a police officer, enters.

JOHAN [*smiles benevolently*]: Tami Walaza. I am sure you are ready to confess now.

TAMI [*stubbornly*]: I told you I have nothing to confess.

JOHAN: For how long do you think you are going to hold on, Tami Walaza? You could be saving yourself all the pain by confessing at once. You know what will happen when the bells toll. [*Laughs menacingly.*] They will come, and they will beat the hell out of you. You owe it to yourself to confess. And go home a free woman. We can even allow you to proceed with your interrupted wedding. Very simple. Confess. Sell your comrades out. They will never know it was you. Confess and go home a free woman.

TAMI: Go to hell, Johan van der Bijl. You'll have to kill me first.

JOHAN: Still stubborn, hey?

He looks at his watch and exits, leaving her alone. Pause. Her eyes register the fear. She is now in a pool of blinding light. The bells toll. She spins around. An unseen force pulls her and throws her on the ground. Then with each toll it hits her in the stomach. She screams and groans in pain. The obscene violence continues until the bells stop. Then there is utter silence while she nurses her pain. After some time she sits up. She looks out and smiles wanly. She stretches her hand out.

TAMI: Oh, little swallow. You have been my only visitor these past weeks. My only companion. Except on Sundays. Torturers are my companions on Sundays. To the sounds of the damned bells.

Ah, you have built your mud nest under the ledge above the barred window. You have come to stay. Until the seasons change and you fly to other climes.

Enter JOHAN, LUTHANDO *and* MZAMO. *Immediately the lovers see each other they try to rush into each other's arms. But* JOHAN *stops them.*

JOHAN: Not so fast. You see, there she is. You can look, but not touch. Maybe when she sees you she will come to her senses.

LUTHANDO: She has told you she knows nothing. She is innocent. Why don't you arrest me instead?

MZAMO: Or me. If there is any terrorist in this town, it is me. I have preached the gospel of 'turn the other cheek', I have preached of a Lord who loves everyone, to whom everyone is equal. I have propagated the treason of equality. I am the terrorist here, not this poor woman.

JOHAN: You are all terrorists. It is about you that she must confess. And she is going to sit here until she confesses.

MZAMO: Give them what they want, Tami. You cannot be a martyr. Tell them what you know, child, and be free.

TAMI: I would rather die.

The bells toll. The pool of light. JOHAN, LUTHANDO *and* NOMZAMO *are on the sidelines. Once more the torture. The violence on* TAMI *with each toll.*

LUTHANDO: I cannot bear this. I confess. I am the terrorist. She had absolutely nothing to do with it. Please stop!

TAMI: He is lying. He had nothing to do with it. He's just confessing to save me.

LUTHANDO: They are going to kill you, Tami. They are prepared to kill you, Tami. Do not be stubborn. You are not a martyr.

TAMI: Let me die, then. If need be let me die.

LUTHANDO: Oh, Tami! Tami!

MZAMO: Tami! Tami!

Lights fade to dark as they scream her name in pain, and as JOHAN *laughs crazily.*

Scene Nine

As the lights rise we discover KATJA *and* MARTIJN. *The barstool that represents Tami's flat is there. But no wine or glass.* TAMI *is not there.*

KATJA: She has changed. She is no longer the same. You must have had a good effect on her.

MARTIJN: If it were really my effect she would be reachable. I can't reach her, Katja. We play the music, we seem to gel, but she's as distant as ever.

KATJA: What is important is that she no longer has what she called the 'demons' that possessed her. You, the music, or both, have exorcised them. She no longer uses wine as a security blanket.

MARTIJN: She was beginning to melt, until she discovered who the Dominee really is. Now she is consumed by anger. I fear she will go back to that wine.

Enter JOHAN VAN DER BIJL.

KATJA: You have the gall to come here after what you have done to her!

JOHAN: Where is she?

MARTIJN: What the hell do you want from her?

JOHAN: Hell doesn't half describe what I have been through.

KATJA: What you have been through? What about what you put her through?

MARTIJN: He hasn't told us what he wants here.

JOHAN: Tami Walaza asked me to ask Catharina and Fritz to join her outfit. I thought she would be glad to hear that they have agreed.

KATJA: Fine, we'll tell her when she comes. Goodbye.

MARTIJN: Close the door after you.

JOHAN: You people, you think you can judge. You don't know half the story.

KATJA: We know that you damaged a young woman and destroyed all her prospects.

JOHAN: She could have rebuilt her life. Many people did. And became even better people because of the very damage that we did to them. They are running South Africa today.

KATJA: That is a good one, isn't it? She was too weak to rebuild herself as others did? It is all her fault. You were doing her a favour when you arrested her at her wedding and tortured her almost to death. You merely wanted her to be a stronger person so that she could run South Africa one day.

KATJA *and* MARTIJN *laugh.*

JOHAN: I do not have to explain myself to you. In my country I went before the Truth and Reconciliation Commission. I revealed all I knew. I confessed to what I did. What is most important to me is that the Commission granted me amnesty. My conscience is now clear. I have started on a clean slate. I have dedicated my life to the work of the Lord. That is why I am here.

MARTIJN: You confessed to your Truth Commission and they forgave you. But did the person you did all these filthy things to forgive you? From what I saw when she came back after talking to you ... after discovering who you really are ... she has never forgiven you.

JOHAN: Tami Walaza was not at the TRC hearing. If she had been there I would have addressed her directly, to ask for her forgiveness.

KATJA: And so, what do you want us to do now?

JOHAN: Nothing. Accept that terrible things did happen ... in good faith, mind you ... no one had any intention of hurting anyone ... accept that things did happen and we, the people of the country, came together to work out our differences. And now we are trying to move forward.

MARTIJN: It may be easy for you to say. But your victim is still haunted by the demons of the past.

JOHAN: I am haunted by the demons of the past too.

Enter TAMI.

TAMI: What is he doing here?

KATJA: He is haunted by the demons of the past, he says.

MARTIJN: He wants to talk to you about them.

JOHAN: I want to make peace, Tami Walaza.

TAMI: And will that bring my life back? Will that restore the life that you stole in its prime?

Enter MZAMO in the second world. He is still dressed in his bishop's maroon. He is a lone figure, almost angelic, in a pool of light. The people in the first world look at him like supplicants as he addresses them. Only TAMI stands defiantly.

MZAMO: Do you swear that you will tell the truth, the whole truth, nothing but the truth, so help you God?

JOHAN [*raising his hand, taking the oath*]: So help me God.

MZAMO: This august body is listening.

JOHAN: It was the past. You cannot hold it against me. The times were times of war. I was a foot soldier. I was used by the elders to fight their war, to do all their dirty work. I carried out their instructions to preserve what they claimed they had created for me ... and my progeny ... and all the future generations ... world without end, amen.

MZAMO: Are you telling this august body that you take no responsibility for your actions? That you blame it all on the elders?

JOHAN: I never really had a life of my own. It was shaped by the elders. I was just clay in the hands of the elders in their grey suits and grey shoes and metallic grey Mercedes Benz sedans. The elders betrayed me. The elders lied to me. Through their Christian National Education and their cultural organisations. They taught me that Tami Walaza was the enemy, that she was bent on eliminating me from the face of the earth. I had to destroy her at all costs. Before she could destroy me. Self-preservation is the law of nature. Blame it on the lies of the elders.

MZAMO: And now you want amnesty? You know the conditions for amnesty: full disclosure and full acceptance of your own guilt and, of course, a political motive for your crimes. You insist that you are innocent, that I should blame it all on the elders. How do I grant you amnesty when you refuse to take responsibility for your actions?

JOHAN: Where are the elders? Why are they not standing here with me? Why should only the foot soldiers face the music?

MZAMO: The elders have melted into the new dispensation. They are now one with it. They are the people who want you to confess and be forgiven. They are part of the people who will forgive you.

JOHAN: They are? I am alone in this? I am sorry, My Lords, it is all my fault. I accept the guilt. I confess. I destroyed Tami Walaza out of my own volition. Out of my own wickedness. Not personal wickedness, but political wickedness. The elders had nothing to do with it. I confess everything I know. I became over-enthusiastic in my duties. I ask for absolution. I ask for amnesty.

MZAMO: This august body is satisfied that you have confessed everything you know. You are absolved. You are hereby granted amnesty. Go in peace, my child.

As MZAMO *exits,* TAMI *runs after him screaming.*

TAMI: No! Come back here, damnit! You cannot absolve him on my behalf! I want justice! At the very least I must be compensated for what I went through. I want justice!

But MZAMO *exits without looking back.* TAMI *turns to* JOHAN *in anger.*

TAMI: Are you happy with yourself now, hey?

JOHAN: It is not my fault, Tami Walaza. You were not there to tell your side of the story. They said you had disappeared in exile. That you had not returned when others were returning. In any case it was not a requirement that I could only be granted amnesty if you, the victim, forgave me. So, even if you had been there, you would not have stopped the amnesty. I did what the law required. I told the truth and was granted amnesty.

TAMI: Whose truth?

JOHAN: Victims had their chance too. They told their truth.

TAMI: And what did they get in return? You got something. You got amnesty. Even if I wanted to sue you for what you did to me it would be impossible, because you got amnesty. What did I get? What did the victims get for their stories?

JOHAN [*earnestly*]: I need your forgiveness too, Tami Walaza. Yes, the government did forgive me. But I'll be happy if you forgive me too.

TAMI: You and your government have forgiven each other. I am not part of that forgiveness.

JOHAN: I should be free. I got the amnesty. But my conscience continues to eat at me. Unlike the elders who were rewarded with big pensions and are enjoying the fat of the land with their smug smiles, I was burdened with a conscience. I turned to God and became his servant. That is why I am here. As a servant of God. I am here because of you, Tami Walaza.

MARTIJN [*obviously feeling sorry for* JOHAN]: Surely, Tami, the man has paid a high price. [*To* JOHAN]: I am sure Tami will forgive you. She cannot hold a grudge for such a long time.

TAMI [*to* MARTIJN]: You stay out of this!

JOHAN: When you get back to South Africa you will see that people are trying very hard to put the past behind them. I hope you too, one day, will learn to forgive.

He exits.

TAMI [*screaming hysterically*]: Oh, no, you don't escape that easily, Captain Johan van der Bijl. We are still having an argument here. You cannot just walk out on me. I want justice. There can be no reconciliation without justice!

She runs after JOHAN *and exits.* KATJA *and* MARTIJN *look at each other puzzled, at a loss about what to do next.*

Lights fade to black.

Scene Ten

Lights rise on the first world. TAMI, KATJA *and* MARTIJN *are sitting or standing around idly.* MARTIJN *is toying around with his little drum, beating some stray sounds. In the third world* HELEEN *enters. She is dressed like St Nicholas.*

KATJA: Heleen is back.

But TAMI *does not make any attempt to move to the window to watch. She just remains where she is. In the third world* JOHAN VAN DER BIJL *enters.* HELEEN *takes out a big chocolate amsterdametje and puts it in* JOHAN's *mouth.*

KATJA: She is tingling his tongue with a phallic chocolate amsterdametje.

HELEEN *strips to her regulation underwear as before. But* JOHAN *is not responsive. She holds the big chocolate and pushes it in and out of his open mouth.*

KATJA: Tami, you should see this. You always enjoy watching this. They are doing it for you. I am sure the dominee is doing for you. He hasn't closed the curtains this time. Perhaps it is a peace offering to you, Tami.

TAMI: When I skipped the country ... went into exile, that is ... my parents didn't even know I was going. I didn't tell them because I knew the police would harass them. For a long time they did not know where I was.

KATJA: It just doesn't look right. Catharina and Fritz are not there to sing for him.

TAMI: And when they died I couldn't go to their funerals. It's a big thing with us, you know? A funeral. I was wandering about refugee camps until a place was found for me here. I missed their funerals ... both of them ... two years apart.

KATJA: It's not the same when Catharina and Fritz are not there to sing for them.

It would seem that JOHAN *and* HELEEN *think so too, they give up their amorous activity in frustration and exit as lights fall on their world.*

KATJA: Damn! They are gone. Without doing anything. She had brought him a St Nicholas gift and had to leave without giving it to him. And it's all your fault, Tami. They can't do a thing without the fanfare that you guys usually make.

TAMI: I have made up my mind. I am going back to South Africa.

This comes as a shock to MARTIJN. *He stops beating the drum.* KATJA *is happy.*

KATJA: Really?

MARTIJN: Just when things are happening for our band? Just when we are beginning to make multi-cultural waves?

TAMI: I have to go back. There is unfinished business back home.

MARTIJN: You can't just leave, Tami. We have commitments to meet, engagements to fulfil. We have gigs lined up!

KATJA: I think she must go, Martijn. It is important that she goes.

TAMI: There are many African women in Amsterdam. I am sure you'll find one who can dance and tell stories. [*Chuckles.*] At least she won't insist on playing a trombone.

MARTIJN: But it is you the people want. You have made a name for yourself and the people want your stories and your dances. You are a black role model, the television man said so yesterday! [*He becomes a television camera man-cum-interviewer.*] 'Smile, Tami Walaza, don't look so glum ...'

TAMI [*laughs at the memory*]: Holland is the least racist country in Europe. Yet it was in this country that I was interviewed by a moron who has internalised all the racist stereotypes of Africa and the Africans you can imagine. Talking to me as if I was an idiot.

MARTIJN *continues to be a television camera man/interviewer.* TAMI *plays along. She sports a broad, toothy, wide-eyed smile reminiscent of a Coon. It is a mechanical smile that stays in place for the rest of the 'interview'.*

MARTIJN: This is television, Tami Walaza. You must come to life when you talk on television. Don't be pensive. You must remember that when you are on television you are a role model for black people who will be watching. When they see a black face on television that black face becomes a role model. Therefore you must be animated. You must laugh. Black people are known as people who laugh. They have the gift of laughter. Be animated. Laugh. Black people have big gestures. Do not be afraid to exaggerate. Use your hands. This is television. And you are a black person. Show you teeth. Good. A bigger smile. Bigger still. Good.

They all laugh.

TAMI: The idiot! It was quite a responsibility I had yesterday, carrying the hopes of the black races of the world on my shoulders!

The bells toll. Nothing happens. TAMI is not attacked by a bout of pain. They all look at her in surprise. She also is amazed. They remain like that for the duration of the bells. When they stop everyone breaks into laughter. TAMI exits in excitement.

MARTIJN: She is cured of the bells!

KATJA: Tell me honestly, Martijn, is it really for the band that you don't want her to go? Or is it for yourself?

MARTIJN: For the band. I must admit, I was interested. But I know when I am in a no-win situation. There could never be anything between us. It is for the band ...

KATJA [*laughs*]: I believe you ... I believe you ...

MARTIJN *beats the drum quite furiously.*

KATJA: I think she must go, Martijn. Let her go.

MARTIJN *beats the drum even harder. Lights fade to black.*

Scene Eleven

Lights rise on TAMI. She is holding her trombone. She blows a few notes as if to call for attention and then addresses an absent LUTHANDO in the second world.

TAMI: Dear Luthando, it's been a long time. But I am coming back. I am on my way back to our beautiful Qhoboshane Valley. You have been silent for a long time. I understand. It would be selfish of me to hold it against you. But, oh, you have been silent for a very long time. Still, I know that wherever you are, whatever you are doing, with whoever you are doing it, you will not forget the promise: to heal the wounded earth!

Enter JOHAN and KATJA.

KATJA: It's a farewell gig. She is going back home. When do *you* go back?

JOHAN: Maybe not at all. There is no place for me in Tami Walaza's South Africa. It is a South Africa of anger, bitterness and vengeance.

Enter HELEEN. She perches herself somewhere between JOHAN and KATJA. It is her red day. TAMI blows a few notes on the trombone again, as if to call her audience to order. She then sings. It is one of South Africa's a cappella songs. Enter from different directions MARTIJN, singing and playing, his drum hung around his shoulder; CATHARINA, using her window cleaning paraphernalia as percussion; and FRITZ holding his easel with a canvas on it. The contribution of the latter two to the song is reminiscent of their singing and humming during Johan's venereal flights. FRITZ has put the painting of a bright sunflower in front of the group as it sings. It will help if the song combines the best of South African and Dutch traditional music. As the song ends, KATJA, HELEEN and JOHAN – comprising the audience – applaud. Lights fade to black.

Scene Twelve

Lights are very dim. TAMI is riding on a bicycle. It is really one of the wire toys that the township kids make, with a wire person perched on it and pedalling as TAMI pushes it. She walks gingerly on a stage strewn with figures huddled together, some squatting, others standing upright or crouching or curling up. She finds her way among them, 'riding' her bicycle. The figures, which are indefinable, are frozen in agony.

THE FIGURES [*singing*]:
Ndophule, ndophule, mntakwethu
(Break me, break me my brother/sister)

> Ndophule, ndophule, ndophule, mntakwethu
> Ndophule mntana ka mame
> (Break me, child of my mother)

She stops next to a figure.

TAMI [*to the figure*]: Please, I am looking for Luthando. Have you seen Luthando?

FIGURE 1: Go find out from that mountain. Maybe it has seen Luthando.

She rides around the stage. Her ride is quite arduous. As she rides the figures sing the same refrain again.

THE FIGURES [*singing*]:
> Ndophule, ndophule, mntakwethu, etc.

She stops next to another figure.

TAMI: Mountains of my beloved Qhoboshane: you with aloes whose nectar makes the birds drunk and spin in the air: have you seen Luthando?

FIGURE 2: Oh, he left these mountains many years ago. They say you will find him in Cape Town. In the Parliament building. We chose him to represent us there. And never saw him again.

She rides again. As arduously as ever. Once more the figures sing Ndophule. *She stops next to another figure.*

TAMI: Luthando? Is that Luthando?

FIGURE 3 [*laughs mockingly*]: Luthando? He has left for Johannesburg. The pickings are richer there. Parliamentarians are too poorly paid. Even though he was the chairman of the defence portfolio committee it was not rewarding enough. He was deployed to the corporate world. He is an executive chairman of a black empowerment conglomerate, which recently won a multi-billion rand tender to supply some defence systems to the army ... in partnership with a Dutch company.

She rides again. The figures sing Ndophule. LUTHANDO *appears, driving a posh Mercedes Benz. It is, in fact, a well-made wire car. He is*

157

obviously enjoying himself, like a township kid driving his toy car, making the sound of the purring and revving engine with his voice, sometimes hooting. TAMI *and* LUTHANDO *see each other, and* Ndophule *stops.*

TAMI: Luthando?

LUTHANDO: Tami! You have returned! You have come back to me. I knew you would come to your senses.

TAMI [*incredulously*]: You waited for me?

LUTHANDO: Waited? I don't think I can call it waiting. But there will always be a place for you in my heart, Tami. We travelled a long road together.

TAMI: What about your cravings for powerful women?

LUTHANDO: Oh, that? It was just a phase. I became a powerful man in my own right, so my craving for powerful women dissipated. Now I find weaker women more attractive. My fetish now is to care for them. Set them up in townhouses and buy them their own little cars. I will set you up too.

TAMI: Oh, is that why you want me? To join your collection of weak women?

LUTHANDO: Oh, no! You are my queen. Their queen as well. You have always been my queen. After all, we were almost married! But first we'll have to pretty you up. There are consultants who will give you a makeover. It's going to be a new you, Tami. [*Pointing at the bicycle.*] But this? What is this?

TAMI: It is a bicycle.

LUTHANDO: Ah, a bicycle. I hear everybody in Holland rides one. But you know, Tami, here a bicycle is the mode of transportation of the lower classes. The lowest class, in fact. So, you'll have to do away with it. I won't begrudge you if you have one for sporting purposes. I can buy you a very expensive mountain bike. [*Emphatic.*] For sporting purposes. But for the purposes of moving from point A to point B it is a no-no.

TAMI: It is the only thing I intend to ride for the rest of my life.

LUTHANDO [*jokingly*]: You can ride me for the rest of your life. There is more pleasure in it. Seriously, though, I cannot be seen by my friends even talking to someone on a bicycle.

TAMI: Your friends will just have to get used to it.

LUTHANDO: You still do want a life with me, don't you?

TAMI: We were almost married.

LUTHANDO: Then you'll have to give up your bicycle.

TAMI: I will not give it up, Luthando. Pedal power! Amandla! It is a healthy mode of transportation. Keeps me fit. No fumes. Keeps the air fresh and clean. You should try it.

LUTHANDO: Are you choosing a bicycle over me?

TAMI: What's happened to you, Luthando? And our vow to heal the broken land? To work with the people to mend the scars of the past? What about the people, Luthando? When we fought for liberation were we not fighting for the people?

LUTHANDO: The people? Who are the people? We are people too, are we not?

TAMI: You have changed, Luthando. The comrades have changed. The camaraderie that used to exist during the freedom struggle is gone. The comrades with whom we worked to develop the community are now involved in self-enrichment activities either as members of the government or of the corporate world. Each person for himself or herself. The erstwhile political and trade union leaders now all have their snouts buried in the trough, trying very hard to outdo one another in piggishness.

LUTHANDO: You live in the past. You will learn soon enough that the good times are not yesterday. They are today. Here and now. We are the makers of history. The creators of a new beautiful society. Democratic. Non-racial. Non-sexist.

TAMI: You have learnt the slogans well.

LUTHANDO: I cannot waste my time talking to you. I have a few committee meetings to attend. A few contracts to broker. I have to collect my brand new Mercedes four-wheel-drive from Daimler Chrysler. They delivered one yesterday. But I didn't like the colour. It does not mean that just because the car is a gift you can take any old colour. So I am on my way to the showroom to choose the colour I want. Good-bye and good luck!

He drives away. TAMI *watches him, then laughs.*

TAMI: I am a victim of the twin diseases of the democratic South Africa: instant gratification and conspicuous consumption.

As she turns to ride away she almost bumps into JOHAN VAN DER BIJL *who entered while she was laughing. He is riding a bicycle similar to Tami's.*

TAMI: You came back after all. Riding your bicycle as elegantly as you rode Heleen.

JOHAN: Heleen's name should not be used in vain.

TAMI: Don't be embarrassed, Reverend. I too have chosen a bicycle over a man. I thought you said you would never come back.

JOHAN: The longing for the smell of the gravel roads after the rain was too much to bear.

TAMI: The call of your ancestors was too strong!

JOHAN: I had a second mission though. To preside over your marriage, as your minister, if you and your fiancé will have me. Since I was the one who destroyed your marriage even before it happened, I want to be the one who joins you together in holy matrimony.

TAMI: You are too late, Dominee. There won't be any marriage. There is something you can do, though. Help me do what Luthando and I had vowed to do: rebuild the scarred land. Heal the wounds that still ache, that history has imposed on my people.

JOHAN: I will be with you. It is not an easy task to heal the wounded earth. But I'll be with you.

TAMI: My loneliness continues. It is like I am still in Europe.

They begin to ride around.

JOHAN: It is the loneliness of freedom.

TAMI: With freedom we need to find a new cohesion. The cohesion of free men and women. We have not found it yet. Apartheid had its own cohesion. When it was destroyed it was as if something had been ripped off one's life. Like a tumour that one had learnt to live with. Now the surgeons have removed it. We look normal and beautiful again. But it is that very beauty that is enfeebling us. Debilitating beauty. We are not used to living a pain-free life. We were addicted to being slaves, now we are suffering from withdrawal. You only have to look at us to see the symptoms. It is painful to be free.

They ride around the stage. The FIGURES *sing* Ndophule. *They are no longer frozen in agony. They are animated. They clap hands joyously. The bells toll. But they are distant. The two cyclists ride in a whirlwind around the stage, laughing. The song also becomes faster. They ride until they collide. Lights fade to dark.*

Printed and bound by CPI Group (UK) Ltd, Croydon, CR0 4YY

13/04/2025

14656582-0005